INTERNATIONAL CYCLES AND
CANADA'S BALANCE OF PAYMENTS, 1921-33

CANADIAN STUDIES IN ECONOMICS

A series of studies sponsored by the Canadian Social Science Research Council, and edited by V. W. Bladen.

1. International Cycles and Canada's Balance of Payments, 1921-33. By Vernon W. Malach.

International Cycles and
Canada's Balance of Payments
1921 - 33

BY

VERNON W. MALACH

UNIVERSITY OF TORONTO PRESS
1954

TO

MY MOTHER AND FATHER

PREFACE

THIS ESSAY is intended primarily as a study of some of the interrelations between cyclical fluctuations and the balance of payments. Most of it was written during the academic year 1947-8 under the supervision of Professor Lionel Robbins at the London School of Economics. I am indebted to him for continual help and encouragement. The University of London accepted an earlier draft of this essay as a thesis in partial fulfilment of the requirements for the Ph.D. (Econ.) London.

I am indebted to Principal W.A. Mackintosh, Professors A.J. Brown, C.A. Curtis, V.C. Fowke, Mabel Timlin, M.C. Urquhart, Jacob Viner, and especially G.A. Elliott, F.A. Knox, and D.C. MacGregor, each of whom read the entire manuscript at one of its stages and made valuable suggestions. They cannot be held responsible, of course, for the result.

I want to express my sincere gratitude to Professor V.W. Bladen and the Editors of the University of Toronto Press for their invaluable editorial assistance, to Miss Daphne Bennett for typing the first manuscript under particularly arduous conditions, and to my wife for aid throughout.

Appreciation must also be expressed for a British Council Scholarship, a Reuben Wells Leonard Travelling Fellowship, a grant from the Queen's University Arts Research Committee, and particularly to the Canadian Social Science Research Council for a generous grant-in-aid of publication.

Vernon W. Malach

Royal Military College of Canada
Kingston, March, 1953

CONTENTS

TABLES

INTERNATIONAL CYCLES AND
CANADA'S BALANCE OF PAYMENTS, 1921-33

CHAPTER ONE

INTRODUCTION

THE PURPOSE of this essay is to fill part of a major gap in the theory of international trade, the international aspects of short-run oscillations, partly by
testing the applicability of various propositions to a concrete case and partly by
testing them for their logical consistency. In this chapter some of the relevant
theories of the business cycle and of the mechanism of adjustment are outlined
and a few comments made. In the next five chapters an attempt is made to
ascertain the applicability of these theories to Canada during the major cycle
1921-33. In the last chapter some summary remarks are made on the consistency
of the hypotheses discussed here.

Perhaps a word of explanation should be given for the number of trade cycle
theories discussed. Those economists brought up on Keynes will no doubt consider
the brief review of other business cycle theories an absurd waste of time. Some
older economists, especially those on other continents, may charge that undue
stress has been given to underconsumption. My purpose has been just this: to
approach the empirical work with an open mind as to the possible applicability
of any particular theory. I feel that to achieve any measure of objectivity one
must not test merely the theory one considers most likely to be applicable. To
do so cannot fail to colour the results. Because of the infinite complexity of
economic phenomena, on occasion one finds evidence to support totally different
theories. Then relative timing of the evidence and a microscopic examination
of all relevant monthly data in the light of various theories are imperative. On
such occasions a person who has started off with the "most likely" theory will
assuredly find exactly what he is looking for and is most unlikely to probe further
to try to disprove the theory which he after all considered beforehand to be the
most applicable. I hope that, upon observing this approach in the following
chapters, the reader will agree that it is well justified.

I. RELATIVE TIMING AND STRENGTH

There appears to be fairly general agreement that the cyclical turning-
points in a country highly dependent upon merchandise exports will lag behind
those in the rest of the world or at least those in her main export markets. Thus
Schumpeter cites England's growing dependence upon foreign trade in the
nineteenth century as a reason why her cycles tended to follow foreign business
situations and her "crises" and financial booms to originate in foreign events.[1]

A second proposition sometimes advanced is that cyclical oscillations in
economically "young" countries will tend to have a wider amplitude than those
in more fully industrialized countries. Thus to explain the behaviour of England's
balance of trade in the nineteenth century Kindleberger advanced the hypothesis that
the young, undeveloped, borrowing countries experienced stronger cyclical move-

ments than England. [2]

Since Canada is both an economically young country and one highly dependent upon foreign trade, her cyclical turning-points, according to these theories, should lag behind those abroad and her cyclical swings should be relatively sharp. We shall find, however, that these expectations are not often fulfilled in the major cycle 1921-33.

II. MECHANISMS OF TRANSMISSION AND ADJUSTMENT

Monetary Business Cycle Theory

This theory attributes industrial fluctuations to variations of bank credit. An increase of the quantity of bank credit induced by a lowering of the bank rate leads to an increase in the volume of merchants' stocks and hence of prices, incomes, and outlay on consumers' goods. Price changes resulting from variations of consumers' outlay [3] have the same effect as further changes of the interest rate. [4]

Under gold standard conditions an expansion in country B, induced by a lowering of the discount rate, would be transmitted to country C (say) through the induced enlargement of merchants' stocks and the increased outlay of consumers in B. The rising prices of B's domestic goods would tend to make foreign goods more attractive and to raise the cost of producing exports. In adjustment to the excess of debits on current account, induced by these pressures, gold would flow abroad. This external drain would combine with the internal drain of means of payment to endanger the banks' cash position and to induce a contractive policy in B which would retard the expansion there. At the same time, the enlarged cash reserves of the banks in the foreign countries receiving the gold would tend to induce easy money policies there and hence cyclical expansions. The expansion at home would thus be transmitted to foreign countries and the rate of expansion in both areas would tend to be equalized. [5]

Monetary Overinvestment or Monetary Undersaving Theory

This theory also stresses the "inherent instability of credit". According to Hayek's original variant of this theory, [6] the rate of interest charged by the banks is determined in the short run by considerations of their liquidity and hence does not necessarily coincide with the "equilibrium" rate of interest which equates the demand for loan capital to the supply of savings. [7] Any divergence between these two rates affords a stimulus to violent movements of investment and hence to the swings of the business cycle. Either a lowering of the market rate of interest by the banks or a rising of the equilibrium rate will cause a discrepancy between the two and bring about a boom by inducing entrepreneurs to deepen the capital structure. But real capital can only be created beyond the limits set by voluntary saving if new bank credits grow faster than consumption expenditure.

While the upswing is the product of credit expansion, the down-turn is usually the product of credit scarcity. The re-emergence of pressure from the consumers' goods industries spells extra competition for credit and for other factors of production. Consumers' demand becomes relatively too high at the same time as supplies of credit and labour become relatively scarce.

The downswing will persist as long as the equilibrium rate is below the market rate. The upswing starts once the banks lower the market rate sufficiently or phychological and technological forces raise the equilibrium rate sufficiently.

Nurkse [8] has presented a relevant international extension of this theory. On the one hand, starting from a position of equilibrium, [9] with a fourfold equality between the market and the natural (equilibrium) rates of interest in countries A and B, Nurkse claims that a fall of the market rate in A resulting from an "artificial" increase of bank credit would lead to internal cyclical expansion and to capital exports to B which would induce expansion there. On the other hand, if the natural rate of interest rose above the market rate in A, capital imports would be induced from B and hence depressive influences would be let loose in the latter country. In the first case marginal investment abroad would be encouraged; in the second it would be discouraged. Thus while in a closed economy a positive discrepancy between these two rates of interest would always lead to an expansionary movement, in an open economy the impulse sent abroad may be vastly different according to which rate moved from the initial position of equilibrium. [10]

Non-Monetary Undersaving Theory

This theory is somewhat similar but does not stress banking activity. Investment--especially in fixed capital--is again the major variable; the rate of interest, its key determinant.

In Cassel's version the low prices for construction materials and low wages resulting from the depression cheapen the production of fixed capital, while low interest rates raise the value of completed capital goods. [11] Conversely, a rising rate of interest leads to a fall in the value of fixed capital; a rise in yield, wages, and the price of investment materials increases the cost of production.

Because of the length of the period of production of fixed capital and the time required for essential enlargement of subsidiary plant, transport, and complementary industries, and for revision of plans and expectations, the reactions produced by these determinants do not make themselves felt at once and hence the fluctuation of fixed capital production extends over a number of years. Technical progress, population growth, and the exploitation of new countries prevent the determinants from effecting even a gradual levelling-out of the trade cycle. The crisis is caused by an over-estimate of the amount of savings available for buying the real capital produced, attributable partly to the fact that these estimates generally have to be made several years in advance of the actual demand for the savings.

Cassel mentions such factors as the exploitation of new countries, immigration and international capital movements as significant variables in the international extension of this theory. But since the behaviour of savings forms its backbone, the cyclical pattern of international capital movements seems to be the most relevant aspect of the international extension.

That there is any cyclical behaviour to long-term capital movements has been denied by Angell. Given cycles of similar timing and strength in two countries, the capital account would not be materially affected by them. With a more rapid expansion in country A than in B, A's relatively high prices would stimulate commodity imports and restrict exports and its relatively high profits and interest rates would stimulate capital imports for investment in fixed-yield securities (the prices of which would be relatively low) and check capital export; and conversely for B. But the relatively high capitalized value of businesses and of shares in A would tend to check the import of capital for investment in such property in A, and conversely in B. [12] Thus A's commodity and capital imports would be positively correlated and similarly for B's commodity and capital exports if investment were only in fixed-yield securities. But capital seeking investment in stocks and direct titles to such property as real estate would be exported from A and hence it would be a question of fact whether the flow of fixed-yield securities predominated to such an extent that the capital account offset the cyclical movement of the trade account. Moreover, interest payments would be relatively constant at any one time and the flow of profit payments would be in an opposite direction to the flow of fixed-yield securities. Hence, taking the situation as a whole, Angell says:

> ... it is evident that there can be no uniform and invariable relation between the net movement of capital and the business cycle, for each phase of the cycle induces important capital flows in both directions. Depending on the international investment situation in the particular case, and on the precise form the investment itself takes, cyclical fluctuations may produce a flow in either direction.[13]

Viner came to "substantially similar conclusions." If a creditor country experienced an earlier or more marked expansion than other countries, domestic interest rates would rise relatively and capital would tend to be invested domestically. Capital exports would suffer at least a relative, if not an absolute, decline; in addition capital imports might occur. Still domestic activity might be correlated with the volume of capital exports.

> ... Given this wide range of possibilities (Viner writes), I see no a priori grounds for expecting to find a significant correlation, whether positive or negative, between the fluctuations in the export of capital by particular countries and the fluctuations in their general level of business activity, unless there is ground for assuming that capital-exporting countries are typically countries whose business cycles always precede or always lag after world cycles, or are countries in which fluctuations in the volume of foreign investment are major factors in initiating fluctuations in the internal level of business activity rather than by-products of the latter. [14]

With this scepticism of two leading authorities as to the cyclical behaviour of capital movements, no straightforward international extension of the non-monetary undersaving trade cycle theory based on such movements appears at first sight. One of the tasks of the following chapters will be to test their scepticism in this vital regard.

Underconsumption Theories

Diametrically opposed to the theory which sees shortage of credit and savings as fundamental causes of the down-turn is the underconsumption theory, which stresses either (1) oversaving relative to the demand for consumers' goods or, more recently, (2) oversaving relative to the level of investment opportunities.

Malthus, J.A. Hobson, Foster, and Catchings were among the leading proponents of the former thesis. They argued that the lower income groups have insufficient income to clear the market of consumers' goods whose supply is being continually enlarged by the increased investment out of the rising savings of the wealthy. [15] An income redistribution would strengthen effective demand for consumers' goods and thus the level of activity.

While these earlier underconsumptionists stressed that too much savings were invested with a resulting overproduction of goods relative to effective demand, Keynes thought the fundamental problem was to get the large volume of savings invested. If only they could be invested, incomes and purchasing power would be increased and there would be no lack of effective demand.

Four major determinants of the Keynesian system are the consumption, investment, and liquidity of preference functions, and the volume of money. The consumption function is of primary importance in determining the "multiplier," i.e., the ratio of the resulting increment of total income to a given increment of investment. If the slope of the consumption function relating real consumption to real income is small, i.e., if consumers spend only fraction of any additional income on consumption, the course of the economy will not likely be explosive. Given an additional increment of net investment and c as the proportion of additional income consumed, national income will increase until $(1-c)$ of the increase of income equals the increment of investment. Hence the increment of income will have to equal the increment of investment multiplied by $\frac{1}{1-c}$, the "investment multiplier."

The second determinant, the investment function, relates the volume of investment to the long-term rate of interest. While Keynes suggested a high interest-elasticity of the investment function, recent theory suggests a much lower interest-elasticity -- especially during depressions. [16]

The investment function and the investment multiplier establish a relation between the level of real income and the rate of interest. The IS curve in Fig. 1 (see p. 10) shows this relationship when the multiplier process has had time to work itself out, i.e., when ex ante [17] savings and investment reach equality. At any given interest rate the marginal efficiency of capital schedule determines equilibrium planned investment; by multiplying this investment with the "multiplier" obtained from the consumption function we ascertain the level of income required to make planned savings equal this planned investment. Thus given the investment and consumption functions, the equilibrium income level can be obtained as a function of the interest rate. A positive shift of either the investment or consumption functions would cause a positive shift of the IS schedule. As long as a fall in the rate of interest increases investment and such increases in investment augment income without raising the rate of interest, the IS curve would retain its negative slope. [18]

The third determinant, the liquidity preference schedule, relates the demand for cash balances to the rate of interest. Keynes assumed the transactions-demand for money to be interest-inelastic and to vary closely with the level of income. The demand for money as a store of value was assumed to vary inversely with the interest rate and to be a matter of the relative advantage at the margin of holding money as against income-yielding assets. These two demands for money combined to form the liquidity preference curve, a functional relationship between money and interest. The fourth determinant, the supply of money as determined by the monetary authority, offers another functional relation between money and the interest rate. The equilibrium money rate of interest is then determined by the intersection of the liquidity preference and the money supply functions.

But the liquidity preference schedule and the supply of money are also involved in a relationship between the interest rate and real income. Given a fixed supply of money and a certain liquidity preference, as income increases the amount of money necessary for "transactions" purposes will rise leading to higher interest rates which will in turn draw idle hoards into the active sphere. Thus with a given quantity of money and given liquidity preference, a positive sloping curve such as LM in Fig. 1 expresses the interest rate as a function of real income when the actual money supply coincides with the amount people wish to hold. As long as the holding of money is safe and costless there is bound to be some positive institutional minimum rate of interest. Hence the LM schedule is likely to be horizontal, or almost horizontal, near the vertical axis. At high income levels the LM curve will be interest-inelastic as sharp interest rate increases finally fail to augment transactions balances.

At E, the point of intersection of the IS and LM schedules, both the liquidity and the savings-investment relations between income and interest are satisfied. [19] These two dependent variables, the IS and LM schedules, are thus simultaneously determined in the Keynesian system by four factors: productivity, thrift, liquidity preference, and the money supply. [20]

If the IS * curve intersects the interest-elastic section of the LM curve, monetary action would be ineffective as a cure for depression. An increase of the money supply (or a decrease in liquidity preference) would mean a positive shift of the LM curve but the new schedule (LM) * would most likely duplicate the exact course of the old one at low levels of national income because of the institutional minimum interest rate. Since the equilibrium position prior to the increase in money, E*, is not changed, national income would not rise and monetary action would be futile.

Keynes believed that conditions in the 1930's were much like these. Since he considered consumption to be a relatively stable function of income, a positive shift of the marginal efficiency of capital schedule appeared to be needed. He concluded that cyclical fluctuations resulted mainly from oscillations in the marginal efficiency of capital. With no "invisible hand" ensuring full employment income, the capitalist economy was left to the whim of such fortuitous forces as population growth, technological change, and the opening up of new frontiers for investment outlets.

Keynes was criticized because he ignored the possibility of investment being induced by changes in the level of consumption expenditure or of total output. But his leading supporters, Harrod, Hansen, and Samuelson, soon corrected this deficiency of combining the acceleration principle [21] with multiplier analysis. Samuelson in particular has shown that cyclical fluctuations will arise from this wedding unless both the marginal propensity to consume and the "Relation" have large values or unless the acceleration co-efficient is relatively small. [22] Another factor besides the acceleration principle which might be responsible for variations in investment activity, namely the size of the capital stock, was noted by Keynes [23] but was not synthesized with the rest of his doctine in such an elaborate fashion as by his followers, especially Kaldor and Kalecki. When these two forces, the acceleration principle and the size of the capital stock, are added to the multiplier, resort need no longer be made to such exogenous factors as bank credit [24] for an explanation of cyclical turning-points.

Another self-limiting factor is the shape of the consumption function. With a marginal propensity to consume less than unity, as income rises a larger and larger amount is devoted to savings and the greater is the need for offsets to these savings to ensure that businesses do not sustain losses. As soon as investment is insufficient to offset these savings a down-turn will result. This last theory, like the multiplier-accelerator and multiplier-capital stock theories, can be paraphrased as a "lack of investment outlets." [25]

The underconsumption theory has a direct and important application in the international sphere. A diminution of foreign demand for a country's exports obviously creates difficulties for that country. Multiplier theory is important here as an explanation not only of a mechanism of transmission of cyclical impulses from abroad but also of one mechanism by which balance-of-payments gaps are closed. [26]

If a stable rate of exchange is assumed, as would prevail under gold standard conditions or under the Bretton Woods agreements, and if merchandise exports rise with no foreign-induced changes in exports or changes in saving, then home incomes will increase and keep on increasing until the demand for imports becomes equal to the supply of exchange made available by current account exports. The larger the marginal propensity to import out of increments of income, the sooner the excess of exports over imports will disappear. On the other hand, the larger the marginal propensity to import, the smaller will be the export multiplier effect on the home economy since the net stimulus of exports will disappear relatively quickly owing to the offsetting effect of import leakages. In so far as part of the increment of incomes is saved, however, the gap will not be fully closed on current account. Ceteris paribus, the larger the multiplier effect, i.e. the primary and secondary enlargement of incomes, the greater will be the measure of adjustment since the larger will be the import demand and hence the smaller the excess of exports over imports. These propositions relate to the increase of home incomes and the mechanism of adjustment which follow from an autonomous increase of exports [27] on income account. In so far as the increase of exports is induced [27] by cyclical expansion abroad, all these propositions still hold, except that no foreign repercussion factor obtains.

The assumptions under which these propositions strictly apply are particularly important. All prices, banking policy, interest rates, and domestic investment activity are assumed constant throughout. In so far as these assumptions do not accord with reality, the effectiveness of this mechanism of cyclical transmission and adjustment may be somewhat diminished or may be reinforced. Thus the gold imports or short-term capital exports resulting from the gap in the balance of payments may induce an expansionary credit policy on the part of the banks which might tend to increase the strength of the cyclical impulse and perhaps also to help close the gap in the balance of payments.

The acceleration principle is particularly important in the international sphere. Domestic investment may be induced by a rise not only of home consumption but also of foreign demand as felt through the export flow. In addition the relative size of the capital stock may be an important determinant of the marginal efficiency of capital in its effect on the ability of merchandise exports to induce domestic investment.

These monetary, monetary undersaving, non-monetary undersaving, and under-consumption trade cycle theories, along with their international extensions, will now be tested for their applicability to the Canadian economy during the 1921-33 period. A relatively complete study of domestic forces will be necessary so that the strength and influence of foreign forces will not be over-estimated.

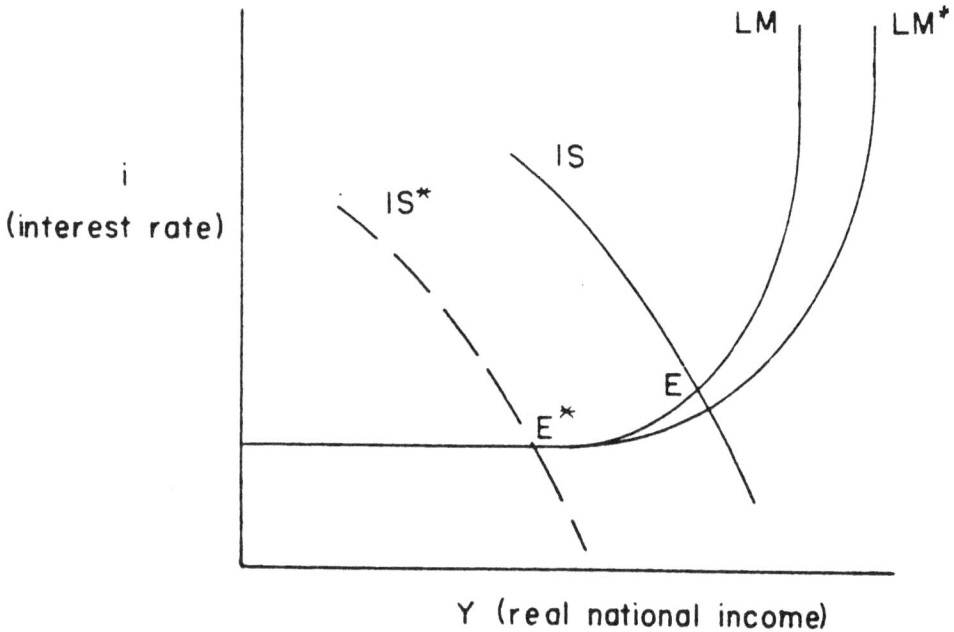

Fig. 1.

CHAPTER TWO

A MAJOR UP-TURN, 1921

THE MAIN FACTORS responsible for the Canadian up-turn in 1921 were the commercial
application of innovations and the early rise of exports. Replacement demand and a
rising rate of growth of consumption may also have been significant. The fall in
money wage and in interest rates seems to have contributed to the up-turn; but on
the whole non-cost factors were more important. Theories stressing monetary
aspects or income maldistribution are less applicable than those stressing the role of
investment. The rise of tourist receipts and long-term capital imports, both mainly
from the United States, were other international factors which may have facilitated
Canada's relatively early up-turn. Despite the influence of the United States,
however, no one foreign country stands out as a predominant source of the revival.

I. TIMING OF CANADA'S UP-TURN

Net national income at 1926 prices [1] fell from $3,702 million in 1920 to
$3,212 million in 1921 and then rose to $3,671 million in 1922 while GNP[2] (Gross
National Product) at 1926 prices rose from $3,756 million to $3,858 million and
$4,511 million. For a more exact determination of the timing, monthly data must
be examined. Seventy monthly series have been studied to ascertain the timing of
the recovery in each. The results are given in Table I. These series have been
selected because of their significance for the economy as a whole.[3] For lack of
adequate general indexes, series on important individual industries have also been
used. To achieve some measure of objectivity, the medians[4] were taken of the
arrays of major cyclical turning-points of the following four groupings: (1) all
series yielding a definite cyclical pattern, (2) all volume series, (3) all
seasonally adjusted series, and (4) all seasonally adjusted volume data.
No great significance can be attached to the fact that the median of all [70] troughs
comes in August 1921. The median of the 57 volume series comes in July 1921 and
of both the 40 seasonally adjusted and 37 seasonally adjusted volume series in May
1921. Thus the application of the two criteria of real terms and seasonal adjustment
points to a trough of Canadian business sometime in the period from May to July 1921.
To be on the conservative side, perhaps the reference date for Canada's cyclical
trough may be placed at the end of this period, in July 1921. [5]

II. CAUSAL FACTORS IN THE UP-TURN

Although the up-turn, as will be seen later in this chapter, occurred relatively
early, it was many years before Canadian activity regained the heights of 1919-20.
The price of No. 1 Manitoba Northern fell from $2.245 per bushel in July 1919 to
$1.13 in November 1921 and occasionally to even lower levels in 1922-4. The
United States emergency tariff promulgated in mid-1921 had a disastrous effect on

11

Canadian exports, especially on fresh and frozen beef, meats of all kinds, preserved milk, butter, and potatoes. But despite these depressing influences, the general level of Canadian activity rose. Our next task is to determine what factors engendered the Canadian revival. Did the primary impulses come from abroad or from favourable domestic conditions?

Current account.[6] Rising export volume and declining import prices were the main factors contributing to the improved current account in 1922, as the following table shows:

CHANGES IN CURRENT ACCOUNT, 1921-2

	In current prices	In 1926 prices *
Receipts	+ $ 82 million	+ $299 million
Payments	- 117 million	- 52 million
Balance	+ 200 million	+ 351 million

* Total current account receipts were deflated by the index of export prices; payments by the index of import prices.

According to the annual data, upward movements occurred in 1921 in two credit items, travel and interest and dividend receipts, but the latter only rose by $0.5 million and declined in 1922. Although the rise of $6.8 million in tourist receipts partly represented a trend movement rather than a cyclical upswing of foreign incomes, it may have been one of the recuperative forces contributing to the Canadian up-turn. Since merchandise and commercial gold exports rose in 1922, they also may have had expansionary effects.

Monthly data are required for more exact conclusions. Hence monthly estimates have been made of Canada's international accounts.[7] According to these estimates only the rise of tourist receipts in 1921 may have contributed to the Canadian up-turn,

Table I
Sequence of Cyclical Troughs in Canada's
Internal Trade, 1921-22 Up-turn [a]

Year	Month	Series
1920	Oct.	Production of foodstuffs*
	Nov.	Dominion of Canada long-term bond prices
		Lead production*[b]
	Dec.	Construction*
		Stockyard hog sales*
		Stockyard calf sales*[c]
		No. of days lost in strikes
		Prices of preferred stocks

Table I (cont' d)

Year	Month	Series
1921	Jan.	Building permits issued (value)*
	Feb.	Average daily electrical output*
	March	Industrial production*
		Volume of business*
		Pneumatic casings produced*
		Consumers' goods production*
		Unemployment in trade unions, <u>inverse</u>
	April	Iron and steel production*
		Manufacturing production*(b)
		Mineral production*(d)
		Forestry production*
		Sheep slaughterings*
		Hog slaughterings*(e)
		Cattle slaughterings*
		Livestock slaughterings*
	May	Production of durable producers' goods*
		Newsprint production*
		Automobile production*
		Employment in mining
		Employment in transportation
	June	Railway freight ton miles
	July	Stockyard cattle sales*
		Livestock marketings*
		No. of shares traded on Montreal stock exchange*
	August	Employment office applications, <u>inverse</u>
		No. of shares traded on Toronto stock exchange
		Prices of common stocks
	Dec.	Employment office placements
1922	Jan.	D.B.S. index of business conditions* (f)
		Employment in manufacturing
		Employment in all industries
		No. of commercial failures, <u>inverse</u>(g)
		Liabilities of commercial failures, <u>inverse</u>
	Feb.	Grain marketings*
		Agricultural marketings*
		Railway passenger miles
		Employment office vacancies
		Employment in construction and maintenance
		Employment in services
		Employment in communications

Table I (cont'd)

Year	Month	Series
		Railway operating revenues
		Wheat receipts*
	March	Production of boots and shoes*
		Coke production*
	April	Distribution*
		Railway carloadings*
		Coal production*
		Employment in logging
		Employment in trade*
		Bank debits* (h)
	May	Pig iron production*
		Production of steel ingots and castings*
		Cold storage holdings*
		Issue of Dominion notes
		Cost of living
	August	Demand deposits
		New bond issues
	Sept.	Wholesale prices
1923	Jan.	No. of strikes (i)
		Current bank loans
	March	No. of employees on strike
	April	Tobacco released for consumption*

* Seasonally adjusted series.

(a) See Appendix D for statistical sources. All production series are physical volume series unless otherwise stated.

(b) Same value in preceding month.

(c) A lower value, 4 months previous, is surrounded by relatively high values.

(d) Index of 27.3 in May 1922 is surrounded by relatively high values; index of 27.4 in April 1921, by relatively low ones.

(e) Same value 4 months previous.

(f) Based on six factors: common stock prices, speculative trading, wholesale prices, business operations, high-grade bond prices, and the sum of the four main classes of deposits with the chartered banks.

(g) June 1922 has a lower (inverted) value but is surrounded by relatively high (inverted) values.

(h) Lower value in February 1923 but this latter value arose from a fuel crisis. See chap. II n.20.

(i) Same value 15 months previous.

since the remaining credit items reached troughs well after the Canadian business up-turn. [8] But when our monthly export estimates adjusted for balance-of-payments purposes are deseasonalized they reveal a trough in July 1921.[9] Hence the rise of total merchandise exports definitely contributed to the Canadian up-turn. [10]

Certain strategic exports had risen before July 1921. According to the unadjusted monthly export data, the troughs of exports of "non-ferrous metals and their products" and of " wood and its products" were the only ones which preceded the up-turn of general business. [11] Exports of aluminum, lead, and electrical apparatus made large gains after May 1921, while those of silver and brass also rose. In the wood group, exports of paper and wood-pulp increased rapidly after June 1921. In the iron group, automobile exports rose continually in the last six months of 1921. These increases in the export demand for aluminum, lead, electrical apparatus, newsprint, wood-pulp, and automobiles must have created favourable expectations in these industries and been conducive to increased investment.

Long-term capital account. The gross long-term capital inflow rose from $267 million in 1920 to $300 million in 1921 and $340 million in 1922, while the gross outflow was $116 million, $154 million, and $100 million in those years. [12] Thus both flows contributed to the $100 million increase in the net balance in 1922. Even in our pessimistic indirect monthly long-term capital estimates, [13] the net import from February to July 1921 was $62.8 million. This inflow may well have facilitated the up-turn in so far as it stimulated domestic investment and the multiplier process.

Balancing account. But it is well known that, when examining the balances of payments, all the accounts must be taken together. The net effect of the current and long-term capital accounts would presumably be found in the remaining items, the monetary gold and short-term capital flows. Even though Canada was not on the gold standard, the banks might have found gold or claims on liquid foreign balances useful reserves for expansion. Any increase in the net claims on foreigners would presumably yield claims on gold in so far as the foreign countries were on the gold standard, and hence might have an expansionary effect on the Canadian banking system. In fact net monetary gold exports totalled $39.5 million in 1921; they reached $28.9 million from February to June alone.[14] At the same time the net external assets of the Canadian banking system fell sharply. Net short-term capital imports as derived from banking statistics totalled $144.4 million in the year ($72.5 million from February to June). That these movements were not mere-seasonal fluctuations can be ascertained by comparison with other years . [15] The net loss of international reserves was relatively great in the first half of 1921 despite the improvement of the current account and the relatively large long-term capital import. Thus no expansionary force resulting from increased liquidity of the Canadian banking system appears here, nor do any primary income or secondary multiplier effects tending to increase Canadian purchasing power and tending to shift demand schedules to the right. [16] With no equilibrating movements of the balancing account [17] the over-all effectiveness of the improvements in the balance of payments just discussed is definitely lessened.

Banking policy. No great expansion of bank credit took place about the time of the up-turn. Total bank loans in Canada fell with only occasional mild oscillations from $1,624 million in September 1920 to $1,204 million in January 1923; [18] total security holdings dropped from $671 million in October 1919 to $310 million in October 1922. [19] The low levels of bank credit, caused to some extent by diminished demand, [20] may be attributed in part to the desire of the banks to work off their advances under the Finance Act. [21] In any case the up-turn was not brought about by increased bank accommodation.

Consumption. The percentage of personal income consumed fell from 106.2 in 1920 to 96.2 in 1921 and then rose to 100.8 in 1922; the percentage of real GNP consumed fell sharply from 90.2 to 84.9 and 83.2 in those years. Computed from the money GNP series the marginal propensity to consume fell from .98 per cent in 1920 to .97 in 1921 and .48 in 1922. [22] The increase in the percentage saved and in the marginal propensity to save which accompanied the up-turn and early upswing was associated in turn with a rapid expansion in investment activity. Gross domestic investment in 1926 prices [23] rose from $410 million in 1921 to $866 million in 1922 -i.e., from 10.6 to 19.2 per cent of real GNP. Of the components of this investment production of producers' and consumers' durable goods and construction seem to have been particularly important in facilitating the Canadian up-turn. The monthly index of the volume of construction rose after December 1920. No monthly index of the production of consumers' durables is available but the production of one important durable consumers' good, automobiles, rose after May 1921, as did the production of producers' durable goods.

But this correlation does not solve our difficulties. Because saving and investment must always and inevitably be equal ex post, and since all statistics relate to the facts ex post, it becomes a fine problem to determine whether the increased savings [24] induced an increase in investment or whether investment was encouraged by other factors and created its own savings by effecting a rise in income. On the one hand, the rise in the percentage saved may mean nothing more than a movement along a stable consumption function as income expanded, as in 1922. [25] On the other hand, it may have been effected by a downward shift of the consumption function, as in 1921. [26] It is significant that this 1921 increase in percentage saved was accompanied by a fall in yield. [27] Although this fall took place long enough before the business up-turn to have aided slightly the early rise of such investment categories as construction and the production of durable producers' goods, it was so small that it can by no means be considered a major factor. Thus the increase in the percentage saved in 1922 seems merely to have been the concomitant of increased incomes and the increase in 1921 was at most a minor factor facilitating the up-turn via its effect on interest rates.

While the rise in the rate of growth of real consumption from minus 3.4 per cent in 1921 to plus 14.7 in 1922 may have helped effect the up-turn, it does not seem to have been the major explanation of investment behaviour. [29]

Innovations. So far rising exports, tourist receipts, and long-term capital imports and consumption growth have appeared as significant stimulating forces with the fall in yield as an additional (minor) factor.

Replacement demand may also have contributed. Net domestic investment in current dollars fell from $656 million in 1920 to minus $74 million in 1921. [30] No doubt this depletion of the capital stock might have helped induce an upward shift

of the marginal efficiency of capital schedule. During the 1930-3 depression net
domestic investment was negative for six years. [31] The annual decrement exceeded
that of 1921 in each of these years but still the recovery was very slow. The speed
of the recovery in 1921 with small disinvestment and its extreme slowness in 1933
despite sizeable capital consumption mean that the extent of disinvestment by itself
does not appear to be an important explanation of the speed of the 1921 up-turn. But
since the previous upswing, 1919-20, was relatively short, no great addition to the
capital stock took place so that perhaps not much disinvestment was necessary to
effect an up-turn.

Innovations were more important in inducing investment, especially in the
automobile, newsprint, electric power, lead and forestry industries. [32] Before 1914
easy access to the techniques and manufactures of the industrial heart of the United
States and the accessibility of cheap water transport had facilitated the growth of
manufacturing in central Canada. Minnesota iron and Pennsylvania coal [33] were
brought behind the moderate tariff wall and combined with limestone from the Niagara
escarpment to produce iron and steel for the rest of Canada. Now came the "New
Industrial Revolution" consisting of the partial switch in manufacturing from coal
and iron to hydro-electric power, oil, and the industrial metals. Central Canada
was rich both in the new water power and in the new raw materials. The new "white
coal" there led to the establishment of electro-chemical and electro- metallurgical
industries such as Carborundum at Niagara Falls. More outstanding was the stimulus
to the two new export staples, newsprint and non-ferrous metals. At the same time,
the potentialities of large-scale production of the automobile plus the attractiveness
of manufacturing in Canada to gain preference in Empire markets encouraged American
automobile manufacturers to set up branch plants in Canada. Moreover, the innovation
of the automobile, which accounts for the increased tourist receipts discussed above,
induced large capital expenditures on the construction of highways, hotels, resorts,
and service centres. Thus the profitable application of basic innovations was a major
factor contributing to the Canadian up-turn via increased investment activity. [34]

Wage rates. The general weighted average of the indexes of wage rates fell
from 207.7 in 1920 to 189.9 in 1921 and 180.2 in 1922. Partly because of rising
productivity [35] and the fall of money wage rates, the index of wage-cost per unit in
manufacturing industries fell from 165.9 in 1921 to 124.1 in 1922. [36] In many of the
durable goods industries the fall in money wage rates alone may have been sufficient
to induce increased investment, in so far as favourable expectations prevailed. [37]
Four factors point to such inelastic expectations. First, the early rise of Canada's
new "staple" exports requiring highly capitalistic methods of production doubtlessly
created sanguine expectations in these industries. Secondly, as discussed above,
opportunities for the commercial application of innovations were relatively great
in such important sectors as the pulp and paper and automobile industries. Thirdly,
the fall in money wage rates in durable goods industries was sharp and generally
occurred within a relatively short period. [38] Thus the harmful effect of slowly sagging
wages, namely the encouragement to entrepreneurs to postpone expenditure increases,
was avoided. Fourthly, improved cost-price ratios arising from other factors encouraged favourable expectations in the construction industry. [39] Thus the fall in

CHART I. REAL CONSUMPTION AND REAL GROSS NATIONAL PRODUCT IN MILLIONS OF DOLLARS, CANADA, 1920-1945.

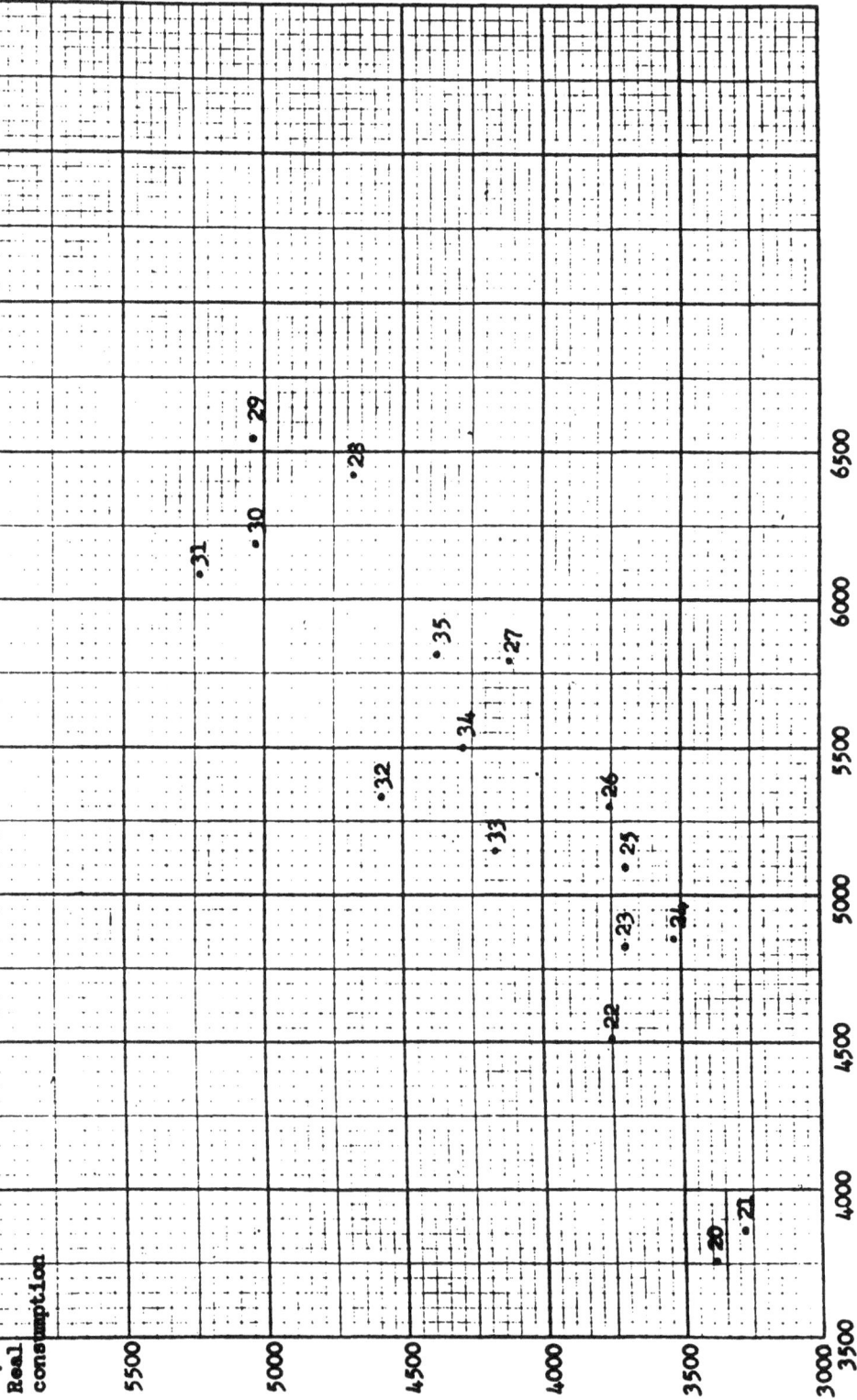

Real consumption

5500

5000

4500

4000

3500

3000

3500   4000   4500   5000   5500   6000   6500

·31   ·29   ·28   ·30

·35   ·27   ·34   ·32   ·33   ·26   ·25   ·24   ·23   ·22

·20   ·21

money wages in the heavy industries may well have contributed to making investment attractive.

Summary. The major factors responsible for the 1921 revival were increased
exports and domestic investment. The major stimuli to the increased investment
were the commercial application of innovations, the early rise of certain strategic
exports, increased tourist receipts, replacement demand, and a sharp rise in the
rate of growth of consumption. Investment expenditure in some of the heavy industries
may also have been induced by a fall in money wage rates coinciding with increasingly
favourable expectations. The large long-term capital import may have had a net
expansionary effect, despite the lack of equilibrating gold and short-term capital
flows, via induced investment. [40] On the whole the Keynesian brand of underconsumption
theory (plus Schumpeter's innovation theory) and the international extension of the
other underconsumption theory are most pertinent in the explanation of the up-turn
although the international extension of the non-monetary overinvestment theory
along with its labour-cost and, to a very minor extent, its interest rate aspects
have limited applicability.

III. THE MECHANISM OF TRANSMISSION OF CYCLICAL IMPULSES

Those expansionary forces which originated abroad are examined further in this
section to ascertain what countries contributed to the revival. [41]

The Canadian up-turn preceded, [42] and her early upswing was more rapid [43]
than, most of those abroad. According to the following troughs of the export flow
to various areas, [44]

United Kingdom	April 1921
France	January 1922
United States	February 1922,

only the rising British demand may have increased the favourableness of expectations
in some of Canada's export industries. [45] But increased demands from other countries
may also have aided Canada's up-turn. The troughs of both exports of "non-ferrous
metals and their products" and exports of "wood and its products" came before that
of business in general. [46] The increased newsprint and wood-pulp exports did not
go to any one foreign market, [47] but increased American demand gave the primary
fillip to expectations in the pulp and paper industry since the United States was
absorbing 72 per cent of Canada's manufactured wood and 88 per cent of her paper
exports. [48] It is impossible to attribute the rise in non-ferrous metal exports to any
one country, [49] but the increased automobile exports during the last six months of
1921 went mainly to "Other Countries" (i.e. to foreign countries other than Britain
and the United States). Since the increased exports of automobiles, non-ferrous
metals, and wood products went to diverse countries, no one country can be credited
with creating expansionary tendencies to these industries. It is true that both the
increased tourist receipts [50] and long-term capital imports [51] came mainly from the
United States. But since no one country was responsible for the increased demand for
Canada's new staple exports, none stands out as primarily responsible for Canada's
early up-turn.

CHAPTER THREE

THE UPSWING

I. DETERMINANTS [1]

The pattern. The first part (1921-5) of the Canadian upswing was on the whole less intense than the American,[2] less intense than most of those abroad, but more intense than the British. The latter part (1926-9) was more intense than the American, British, and most of those abroad. [3]

External factors. In 1921-5 the current account became, on the whole, progressively more active as merchandise exports rose relative to imports. In 1926-9 the current account balance became more passive owing to the sharp and continued rise in merchandise imports.

The combination of fluctuating world demand and inelasticity of world supply produces sharp variations in the prices of many of Canada's main exports. Moreover, the vagaries of nature render the volume of some of the principal exports, primarily grain, unpredictable. In 1921-4 small export volume and low prices spelled a state of relative depression for many of Canada's export industries, especially wheat and livestock, and contributed to the lethargy of Canada's upswing. The sharply rising incomes of the later twenties were the result largely of a high and stable level of export [4] activity plus moderately high export prices.

On the whole the pattern of the Canadian upswing cannot be explained to any significant extent either by the direction or by the strength of long-term capital flows. [5] And the monetary gold and short-term capital flows seemed to have been determined by relative cyclical movements, and not to be independent variables determining the rate of domestic expansion. [6]

The geographical sources of the long-term capital imports and merchandise exports are of interest. It was primarily American capital which bolstered Canada's expansion in certain years of the upswing. Merchandise exports to Britain, America, and Other Countries all contributed to the gradual rise of total exports in 1921-5. Rising exports to America and Other Countries offset falling exports to Britain to leave total exports relatively stable in the latter half of the upswing.

Although the level of British income was the most important determinant of British merchandise imports from Canada, other factors were also important. This conclusion is not surprising since Canadian exports to Britain were mainly for the production of non-luxury consumers' goods which usually have low elasticities of demand with reference to both price and income. A relatively low income elasticity of British demand for Canadian exports is consistent with the fact that the volume of exports to Britain remained relatively stable throughout the latter part of the upswing, generally speaking, although British national income continued to increase. The small fluctuations in volume which actually did occur at this time may have arisen, in part, from the influence of competitive prices. Although the price elasticity of demand for such goods is usually relatively low, the price elasticity of demand for

imports from any one individual exporting country may be relatively high if competition
is effective. Thus any attempt to maintain a price for Canadian wheat sufficiently
different from that of similar foreign wheat would result in a relatively great change
in the volume of Canadian wheat taken.

The relatively close correlation between American income and imports from
Canada is explained partly by the fact that these goods consist mainly of newsprint
and such producers' goods as non-ferrous metals, the demand for which tends to
respond strongly to fluctuations in American activity. In addition the degree of
competition in the markets for those exports going to America does not seem to have
been as high as in the markets for those going to Britain. The geographical proximity
of complementary resources and monopolistic elements in such important export
industries as minerals and newsprint would appear to have been contributing factors
to this relative market imperfection. These monopolistic elements seem to have
been partly responsible for the relative stability of the prices of exports going to
America. And greater price stability together with greater income elasticity of
demand helps to explain the closeness of the relationship between American income
and imports from Canada, as compared with the relationship between British income
and imports from Canada.

On some occasions the close dependence of Canadian prosperity on that of the
United States has been denied. Perhaps nothing in the above analysis proves that
they are very closely related, but the spilling over of a fairly regular, even if small,
proportion of American income must be considered a reasonably important factor
affecting the level of Canadian activity. The regularity with which American demands
spilled over into Canada, despite the erection of high American tariffs, reminds one
of the penetration of strong local cyclical movements into the remaining regions of
any one country.

Moreover, increased exports to America probably were more stimulating to the
Canadian economy than were increased exports to Britain. In addition exports to
America induced considerable investment throughout the upswing in what are
intrinsically capital-intensive industries. Investment in the pulp and paper and non-
ferrous metal industries led in turn to increased investment in other capital-intensive
industries such as construction materials, explosives, chemicals, electric power,
electrical equipment, and machinery. On the other hand, the increased wheat and
animal exports to Britain do not seem to have stimulated an investment boom of
similar proportions. First, expansion in the Prairie region was not resumed until 1925,
while the newsprint expansion appears to have been fairly well sustained throughout
the 20's. Secondly, the production of vegetable and animal exports was, by its very
nature, not as capital-intensive as the new export industries springing up in the
Laurentian Plateau and in British Columbia. Thirdly, the newsprint and non-ferrous
metal industries were new. The large investment in fixed capital in these industries
required the simultaneous development of similarly capitalistic subsidiary industries
while those subsidiary to farming had already been fairly well established in the
1900-13 period. Hence it appears that the total expansionary effect of increased exports to the United States may well have been greater than that of increased exports
to Britain throughout the upswing as a whole. This conclusion does not, of course,
mean that Canadian prosperity was a function of the level of American activity alone.

It is sufficient to point out the single fact that the Canadian upswing did not proceed at a rapid rate until most sectors of the economy were undergoing a relatively strong expansion. A high level of national income was not attained in Canada until, for example, the price of wheat and allied products rose sufficiently in 1925 to make Prairie expansion once more economical.

Major domestic determinants. According to the multiplier and accelerator theory, as income rises because of augmented investment and exports, consumption also rises and thus encourages additional investment in the consumers' goods sector and those industries equipping this sector. But despite rising national income and GNP, consumption both in real and in money terms fell in 1923-4. [7] Downward shifts of the function relating consumption to income payments to individuals were mainly responsible for similar shifts in the function relating consumption to GNP, both in real [8] and in money terms, in 1923-4. The relative stability of the latter function in 1925-8 and its upward shift in 1929 greatly facilitated the expansion based on high exports and rising investment.

While domestic investment throughout the upswing was partly autonomous [9] and not induced by a previous rise of merchandise exports or of GNP, still the low level primarily of exports and to some extent of consumption expenditure [10] was responsible for only a gradual rise of home investment in the first half of the upswing. Construction contracts awarded fell from $332 million in 1922 to $276 million in 1924; [11] and total dwellings completed in Canada fell in 1924, [12] as did the production of "producers' and consumers' durables." The maintenance of a high level of exports in the latter half of the upswing, on the other hand, encouraged large domestic investment and thus brought about high levels of GNP.

Conclusion. The behaviour of merchandise exports and domestic investment seems to be most important explanation of the pattern of Canada's upswing. With a low level of exports in the first half of the upswing, and resulting low level of induced domestic investment, Canada's GNP rose very slowly. The high level of exports in the latter half of the upswing plus the high level of induced investment combined with the autonomous investment to create very high income levels. Consumption expenditure also contributed to this pattern by falling in 1923-4 and rising continually in the latter half of the upswing. All three determinants had to reach high levels before high levels of employment or national income were achieved.

II.   MECHANISM OF ADJUSTMENT [13]

During the period of 1922-5 Canada's upswing was generally less intense than those abroad and the consequent rise of merchandise exports relative to imports rendered the current account balance on the whole progressively less passive or more active. During the period 1926-9, on the other hand, Canada's upswing was generally more intense than those abroad and the resulting rise of merchandise imports relative to exports made the current account balance progressively less active or more passive. The current account was the major independent variable in Canada's balance of payments. The major adjusting force in both halves of the upswing is seen below to have been the balancing movement of long term capital

responding mainly to differences in the speed of business expansion at home and
abroad. [14]

Major independent variable. Correlations of both the yearly and the monthly [15]
international account estimates with the exchange rate point to the current account
as the major factor in the balance of payments, i.e., the marginal force mainly
responsible for the exchange rate movements and tending to set the tune for the
remaining international account items. On the whole the fluctuations of the current
account were a product of the relative speeds of cyclical expansion at home and
abroad. Thus merchandise exports rose relative to imports in 1921-5 when expansions
abroad were more rapid than Canada's. With a low level of induced investment because of the low level of exports, Canada's need for American capital goods [16]
was small; with a low level of income the demand for foreign luxury goods was small.
Merchandise imports rose relative to exports in 1926-9 when Canadian expansion was
more rapid than those abroad. With a high level of investment then, induced in part
by the high level of exports, Canada's need for American capital goods was very
great-- as was her demand for foreign luxury goods resulting from the high national
income. Since the major factor in Canada's balance of payments was thus not a
product of the remaining international accounts, [17] but rather of the relative speeds
of expansion at home and abroad, it may be considered the major independent
variable in the balance of payments throughout the upswing as a whole.

Adjustment processes, 1922-5. [18] In short-run adjustment to the increased merchandise exports, the Canadian dollar appreciated in each of these years except 1923,
net short-term capital exports [19] occurred in every year except 1922 and net imports of
monetary gold in every year except 1923. Import prices behaved as expected in
every year but 1925 by following the Canadian price of the American dollar. In so
far as export prices were even partly set domestically, more favourable terms of
trade would be expected in 1922, 1924, and 1925 providing no autonomous price
movements occurred. In fact they became more favourable in 1924 and 1925 and
less in 1923 but also in 1922, which is hardly surprising in view of the sharp independent
fall of export prices. The variations of export prices seem to have been the product
of independent price movements on world commodity markets rather than of exchange
rate or domestic price fluctuations. Thus all parts of short-run adjustment behaved
as expected with the minor exceptions noted.

The increased merchandise exports caused a primary and perhaps also a secondary
income expansion (via multiplier and accelerator effects). Moreover, the favourable
turn of the terms of trade in 1924-5 offered a definite inducement to increase merchandise imports. Bank loans, however, did not contribute toward adjustment. Despite
the relatively large monetary gold imports, the cash reserves of the chartered banks
fell as the banks paid off [20] advances under the Finance Act and loans decreased
throughout the 1922-5 period. [21] Thus no secondary purchasing power expansion
through increased bank credit took place. Nor did any strong forces arise from bank
action tending to inflate domestic prices.

But despite the primary income effect, the secondary (multiplier-accelerator)
income effects and the relatively low import prices resulting from the appreciation
of the Canadian dollar, all arising from the credit surplus in the current account

(which was significantly large only in 1924-5), merchandise imports fell in 1924 and by 1925 were $13 million below the 1923 level. This was partly the result of a change in income distribution. [22]

A greater measure of final adjustment was provided through international differences in the speed of cyclical expansion acting on the long-term capital account. With the American upswing relatively rapid, Canadian net long-term capital imports fell in 1923-4 and a net export appeared in 1925. New issues of Canadian securities abroad exhibited a downward trend; net purchases of outstanding securities and maturities and redemptions rose every year. [23] Despite this strong equilibrating movement of the long-term capital account, final balance-of-payments equilibrium was not achieved in so far as this outcome implies no further need for balancing movements of monetary reserves.

Adjustment processes, 1926-9. In response to the large and sustained rise in merchandise imports in the latter part of the upswing, the Canadian dollar fell in 1927-9, monetary gold exports occurred in every year except 1927, and short-term capital imports in every year except 1926. Thus the short-run adjustment expected under gold standard conditions occurred on the whole.

The increased merchandise imports exerted a primary and perhaps also a secondary (multiplier-accelerator) income contraction. But no secondary purchasing power contraction took place by way of a reduction of bank loans. Despite the loss of international reserves a sizable secondary expansion of means of payment took place, facilitated by the Finance Act, 1923, under which the banks could obtain Dominion notes seemingly without limit. As the demands for American exchange to buy American capital goods grew larger, the bank presented Dominion notes to be exchanged for gold for export. Their cash reserves being thus depleted, the banks replenished them by borrowing Dominion notes under the Finance Act. Even after the Department of Finance refused gold for Dominion notes presented in January 1929, thus effecting a gold export embargo, the banks continued to borrow Dominion notes to assist the domestic credit expansion. [24] No relative contraction of bank credit occurred and hence no adjustment here to the balance-of-payments gap either through income or price changes. Still the rate of increase of purchasing power may have been diminished somewhat by a relative slackening of demand for credit as the continued growth in physical capital in the face of constant exports lowered the marginal efficiency of capital [25] in certain industries.

The turn of the terms of trade against Canada in 1928-9 resulted mainly from independent movements of international goods prices, not for the reasons suggested by "classical" mechanism of adjustment theory. Since domestic prices rose relatively to import prices, no strong equilibrating fall in import demand resulted. Importing was made more attractive as the intense creation of credit tended to raise domestic prices.

Important balancing movements occurred in the long-term capital account. The high level of new issues and direct investment, 1926-9, the continual decrease in net purchases of outstanding securities, 1927-9, [26] the decline and reversal of insurance capital exports, and the decline of maturities and redemptions in 1927 and 1929, were all brought about at least partly by relative cyclical conditions.

With a high level of domestic investment and an insufficiency of domestic savings, foreign funds had to be tapped, although not to the extent necessary in former years. Net long-term capital moved strongly in a balancing direction in 1926 and especially in 1929 when the debit gap in the current account was sizable. [27]

But the strong balancing movement of long-term capital did not close the balance-of-payments gap caused by Canada's intense upswing. Monetary reserves were exported at an increasing rate and some adjustment was achieved by fluctuations of the exchange rate beyond the gold points thus rationing the relatively scarce American dollars. Canada abandoned the gold standard rather than abandon prosperity.

Summary. The short-run adjusting forces expected under paper standard conditions were generally in operation in 1922-5; those expected under gold standard conditions were found in the main in 1926-9. The major disturbing factor in Canada's international accounts, the current account, and the major equilibrating factor, long-term capital, seem to have had a common cyclical origin. But adjustment was incomplete in 1922-5 despite primary and secondary (multiplier-accelerator) income effects and favourable price changes--partly because of the contraction of bank loans and the changing income distribution. In 1926-9 adjustment was again incomplete despite an orthodox turn of the terms of trade, primary and secondary (multiplier-accelerator) income effects, and possibly a decrease in the marginal efficiency of capital at the very end of the boom--partly because of the expansion of bank loans. The influence of these adjustment processes on the level of imports was not strong enough to counterbalance the basic influence on imports of the relative level of Canadian acitivity, which was low because of low exports and low investment in 1922-5 and high because of high exports and domestic investment in 1926-9.

CHAPTER FOUR

A MAJOR DOWN-TURN, 1929

THE IMMEDIATE DEPRESSING INFLUENCES mainly responsible for the early
Canadian down-turn were the buyers' strike in wheat and the decline of investment
opportunities. Wage increases in the construction industry may have contributed, but
only slightly. On the whole the Keynesian brand of underconsumption is found to be
more applicable than undersaving, monetary or other underconsumptionist theories.

I.   TIMING OF CANADA'S DOWN-TURN

The medians of the peaks derived from all 70 monthly series, [1] from the 43
seasonally adjusted series, from the 57 volume series, and from the 37 seasonally
adjusted volume series came in May 1929. Thus close agreement is evidenced. All
four medians point to May 1929 as the Canadian cyclical peak. The belief held in
many Canadian circles that there was a Canadian down-turn in the autumn of 1929
hardly appears justified since most of the important sectors of the economy had
already experienced a recession of activity many months before this date. [2]

II.   CAUSAL FACTORS IN THE TOWN-TURN

The popular conception of a Canadian down-turn in the autumn of 1929 is based
sometimes on the fact that the American stock market crash occurred in October and
sometimes on the belief that a fall in exports resulting from the small 1929 wheat crop
diminished the purchasing power of the farming community. The depressing effect of
neither of these factors is to be underrated; but since the Canadian down-turn appears
to have come earlier than commonly supposed, one must look elsewhere for its
fundamental explanation. [3]

Current account. In so far as the deterioration of Canada's current account balance
seems to have resulted largely from a domestic expansion more intense than those
abroad it was induced by relative income movements and need not have been a
major depressing influence. Gross investment in 1935-9 prices rose continuously
from 1926 to a peak of $1,180 million in 1928, [4] for an increase of real domestic
investment more than offset the fall of the current account. In 1929, however, real
gross investment fell sharply to $1,012 million because of a sharp fall in the
current account balance; real gross domestic investment, both including and excluding inventories, continued to rise.

Table II
Sequence of Cyclical Peaks in Canada's
Internal Trade, 1929-30 Down-turn [a]

Year	Month	Series
1928	Jan.	Dominion of Canada long-term bond prices
	Aug.	Railway passenger miles
	Sept.	Unemployment in trade unions, inverse
		Employment office vacancies [b]
		Employment office placements [b]
	Oct.	Railway operating revenues
		Railway freight ton miles
		Agricultural marketings*
		Grain marketings *
		Wheat receipts*
		Pneumatic casings produced*
	Dec.	Pig iron production*
		Employment office applications, inverse
1929	Jan.	Production of durable producers' goods*
		D.B.S. index of business conditions*
		Volume of business*
		Industrial production*
		Construction*
		No. of shares traded on Toronto stock exchange
		No. of shares traded on Montreal stock exchange*
	Feb.	Coal production*
		Prices of preferred stocks
	March	Iron and steel production*
		Automobile production* [c]
		Building permits (value)*
		Bank debits*
	April	Consumers' goods production*
		Mineral production*
		Manufacturing production*
		Railway carloadings*
	May	Forestry production*
		Distribution*
		No. of strikes
		No. of days lost in strikes
		No. of employees on strike

Table II (cont'd)

Year	Month	Series
1929	June	No. of commercial failures, <u>inverse</u>
		New bond issues
		Stockyard calf sales*
	July	Stockyard cattle sales*
		Livestock marketings*
		Cattle slaughterings*
		Hog slaughterings*
		Livestock slaughterings*
		Production of steel ingots and castings*
		Employment in transportation
	Aug.	Retail sales*
		Employment in all industries
		Employment in manufacturing
		Employment in construction and maintenance
		Wholesale prices
		Production of foodstuffs*
		Stockyard hog sales*
		Coke production*
		Average daily electrical output*
		Dominion notes in hands of the public*
		Liabilities of commercial failures, <u>inverse</u>
	Sept.	Employment in services
		Demand deposits*
		Prices of common stocks
	Oct.	Production of boots and shoes*
		Current bank loans*
		Employment in communications
	Nov.	Employment in mining
		Newsprint production*
	Dec.	Employment in logging
1930	Jan.	Cost of living
	Feb.	Lead production*
	May	Tobacco released for consumption*
		Cold storage holdings*
	July	Employment in trade*

* Seasonally adjusted series.
(a) See Appendix D for statistical sources.
(b) Higher value 12 months previous.
(c) Higher value 7 months previous is surrounded by relatively low values.

Four categories of current account receipts [5] fell in 1929: merchandise exports, freight, non-monetary gold, [6] and "other credits." The total fall was quite large as shown in the following table:

CHANGE IN CURRENT ACCOUNT, 1928-9

	In current prices	In 1926 prices
Receipts	-$142 million	-$113 million
Payments	+ 137 million	+ 184 million
Balance	- 279 million	- 297 million

The peaks of both merchandise exports and freight receipts in our monthly balance of payments came in November 1928. When this export series is deseasonalized, the cyclical export peak comes in July 1928, as does the cyclical peak of the volume index of exports. According to our deseasonalized estimates, exports remained at a fairly high level until April 1929. In May they fell sharply, remained relatively low in June and July, and then fell even more sharply in the rest of the year. The sharp fall of exports in May 1929 seriously disturbed not only the farming population but also the business community. On a "Black Tuesday" early in May there was a sharp break in prices on the Winnipeg Grain Exchange. Expecting January winter storms in Russia and America to cause severe damage to the winter wheat crop. speculators had forced up the price of wheat. But it became obvious that no damage had occurred. With a large winter wheat crop, plus the huge surpluses from the 1928 crop, Europe refused to buy at the artificially high price. [7] It was considered reasonably clear that the congestion in grain would curtail business in Western Canada, and to a lesser extent in the East, for some months at least. The prospects of reduced purchasing power because of lower returns on 1928 crops together with the increasing certainty of Hoover's tariff aggression [8] undermined business confidence. The danger that another bumper crop would further aggravate the overproduction of wheat and reduce Western purchasing power even more induced many manufacturers, for example, Ford of Canada, to curtail production substantially.

This European buyers' strike was largely responsible for the decline of exports of "vegetables and their products" after November 1928 below their regular seasonal pattern. After July 1929, when the certainty of a poor Canadian crop and the possibility of poor Australian and Argentine crops inspired even more selling restraint on the part of the Wheat Pools [9] and private grain interests and induced the general public to speculate heavily in wheat, Winnipeg prices went up faster and further [10] than those anywhere else and the buyers became even more adamant. Canadians thought their wheat should maintain its premium over other wheats because of the high protein content usually found in dry year crops [11] but foreign millers economized on Canadian wheat once its price became too excessive and used others. [12] The Dominion Government's chief grain official, Mr. Ramsay, urged Canadians to hold on to their wheat until adequate prices were secured. The Government seemed anxious to avoid further curtailment of the West's purchasing power. But by October .

hundreds of farmers had no returns from their crops and in Sasketchewan alone over 5,400 farming families without funds were deemed dependent upon Government aid for survival over the winter. [13]

Two other export categories reached peaks before Canada's business cycle peak; "animals and their products" and "iron and its products." [14] Significant declines occurred in only two major iron product exports, farm equipment and vehicles. These declines may have been partly responsible for the decline in iron and steel production and in automobile production after March 1929. [15] The fall of exports of "animals and their products" seems to have reflected mainly rising domestic consumption and rising domestic prices.

Long-term capital account. The total inflow of long-term capital in 1929 was $349 million compared with $357 million in 1927 and $242 million in 1928. The increased inflow together with the sharp fall in the gross outflow from $346 million in 1928 to $163 million in 1929, transformed the net movement from an outflow of $104 million to a net inflow of $186 million. [16] According to the monthly indirect estimates, net long-term capital imports during the first six months of 1929 totalled $143 million, the largest import for the similar period since 1920. This large long-term capital import is also evidenced in the series on new capital imports from the United States. These totalled $223 million in the first half of 1929. In neither series did a sharp decline occur until after July 1929. Hence no pressure appears to have come upon the Canadian economy from any cessation of long-term capital imports. Rather, these imports were waxing exceeding large and thus may have tended to facilitate a continued expansion of Canadian business.

Banking policy. Despite the loss of international reserves [17] the banks did not contract credit during the first six months of 1929. The peak of the seasonally adjusted index of aggregate issues of Dominion notes came in June 1929, [18] of notes in the hands of the public in July, and of demand deposits in September. The total of notice and demand deposits by the public in Canada reached a peak in October 1929 as did total loans in Canada. The peak of the seasonally-adjusted index of call loans in Canada occurred in July 1929; that of current loans in October. [19] Clearly the loss of international reserves [20] by the commercial banks did not lead to any curtailment of credit. The peak of monthly average daily advances under the Finance Act came in November 1929. [21] Thus neither the commercial banks nor the Department of Finance seems to have attempted to curtail credit. Durbin's theory of a deliberate imposed contraction of credit as the basic causal force of the down-turn does not apply.

The rates charged on borrowings from the commercial banks seem to have remained relatively stable; [22] the rate charged by the Department of Finance to banks on Finance Act advances remained unchanged from September 1, 1928, to October 26, 1931. [23] Thus Hawtrey's theory of the depressing effect of a rise in the short-term rate of interest does not apply either. Clearly the Canadian down-turn was not precipitated by any internal banking action.

Consumption. Nor was the down-turn effected by a falling marginal propensity to consume. The unrevised GNP estimates converted into real terms (Fig. 2) indicate a rise in the marginal propensity to consume from .74 in 1927 to .88 in 1928 and a fall to 28.0 in 1929-- .70, .56 and 20.0 according to the revised 1952 series; [24] and 1.12, .88 and 6.63 according to the new disposable income data. Because of the shift [25] in the consumption function in 1929, however, the marginal propensity computed from the annual increments seems too crude a criterion for this year. We are left with a falling marginal propensity to consume in 1928 when the revised 1952 D.B.S. estimates are used. But because of the upsurge of consumption in 1929 it is impossible to attribute the business down-turn to any decline in the marginal propensity.

While the rate of increase of real consumption was only 3.9 per cent in 1929 compared with 8.6 and 6.8 per cent in 1927 and 1928 an upward shift of the consumption function raised the percentage of real GNP consumed from 66.5 in 1928 to 69.0 in 1929 and the percentage of disposable income consumed from 92 in 1928 to 95.7 in 1929. The rate of growth of real GNP fell even more sharply than that of real consumption plus exports in 1929--doubtless partly because of a fall in induced investment. [26] Real exports may have been more important than domestic consumption in effecting this fall in induced investment since they fell sharply while consumption rose quite strongly considering the minute increase in GNP. Since the fall in the rate of growth of consumption may well have been largely a result of the minute rise in disposable income or GNP since the marginal propensity to consume did not fall in 1929, and since the percentage consumed (and the consumption function) rose sharply in 1929, on the whole there is no evidence here for an underconsumptionist explanation of the down-turn in the form of inadequate demand for consumers' goods.

The monthly retail sales support this conclusion since their seasonally adjusted index rose sharply from 108.8 in May to a peak of 114.4 in August 1929 and remained stable at 114.2 and 114.3 in September and October. Thus domestic consumption rose sharply with the feverish speculation in wheat in the middle of the year, after the Canadian cyclical down-turn, and then remained at a high level for several months. [27]

Because of the sharp fall in the percentage saved [28] associated with the upward shift of the consumption function, the possibility of an undersaving explanation of the down-turn must be examined seriously. [29]

Yield. The rise of the long-term interest rate from 3.78 per cent in January 1928 to 4.41 in June and July 1929 might seem to have been an important factor curtailing investment, but the evidence for this hypothesis is not as satisfying as it might appear at first glance. [30] The rise of 0.36 percentage points in the long-term rate of interest, 1928-9, seems too moderate [31] to be taken as proof of an insatiable demand for capital bidding its price up to extreme heights. Secondly, if a capital shortage was the plague which scourged our industries, made them give up capital projects, and thus reduce employment, incomes, and consumption, it would be reasonable to expect some business men at least to identify it clearly. Thirdly, while the financial papers occasionally mention a tightness of money, they also emphasize that there was no shortage of funds for legitimate ventures not connected with stock market speculation. Fourthly, no strong price inflation took place. [32] Domestic undersaving was not responsible for the down-turn.

Wage rates. Labour scarcity is only a slightly more tenable hypothesis. The index

of employment rose sharply from 104.6 in 1927 to 111.6 in 1928 and 119 in 1929.
"Unemployment in trade unions" reached a trough of 2.2 per cent in September 1928
compared with a trough of 1.8 in September 1919. But most wage rates did not rise
sharply [33] and the index of unit wage-cost in manufacturing industries actually declined from 90.4 in 1928 to 88.6 in 1929 [34] partly perhaps because of slightly
increased productivity. Only the wage rate index for building trades showed a very
sharp rise. [35] In so far as the rise in the costs of building and construction materials
from an index of 96.0 in March 1928 to a peak of 100.6 a year later may have induced inelastic expectations, this sharp wage increase may have been partly responsible for the decline in construction activity after January 1929. Despite this
depressive influence on the construction industry, however, it is difficult to believe
that these generally moderate wage increases were mainly responsible for the
Canadian down-turn. [36] On the whole they probably were more important in
maintaining consumption expenditure than in slashing profit margins.

Investment opportunities. The thesis that a dearth of investment opportunities
may have caused the down-turn seems to be more applicable. A definite worsening of
expectations occurred in pulp and paper, [37] which was one of the prime movers of
the Canadian up-turn and upswing. In 1928 and 1929 only 82.4 and 85.1 per cent
of newsprint capacity was being utilized. Yet most of the mills were capitalized
for a production of from 90 to 100 per cent of capacity. Current construction meant
that the capacity of the industry would be even larger once existing projects were
completed. [39] Clearly this was a situation which was not likely to continue very
long. At this point the newsprint industry was forced to take a substantial price cut [40]
--partly because of Swedish competition. This blow coming at the end of the
gestation period would appear to have been one of the major factors responsible for
the decline of construction contracts awarded and of the production of durable producers'
goods in the first quarter of 1929. [41] Since pulp and paper uses much electricity,
another of the innovating industries was thus also struck. This deterioration of expectations in the innovating industries must be considered a major cause of the
Canadian down-turn.

Summary. The deadlock in wheat and the decline of investment opportunities
seem to be the major causes of Canada's early down-turn. Before these two problems
could be solved the rest of the world had also suffered set-backs so that what might
have been but a minor recession for Canada developed into a major depression.

The fall of construction activity after January 1929 may have been induced
partly by rising labour and material costs. But more important was the lack of
profitable investment opportunities, especially in the pulp and paper and electric
power industries but also in the automobile, farm implement, and wheat industries.

Thus the Keynesian brand of underconsumption theory is particularly applicable
to the 1929 down-turn. So also is Robertson's theory of structural change and
capital glut. Basic structural changes resulting from the application of science to
agriculture and of innovations to Canada's manufacturing and transportation industries
caused a glut of capital goods relative to the demand for their products not only in
the wheat and pulp and paper industries but also in railways, electric power, and
iron and steel. The down-turn was not effected by any shortage of savings, domestic

or foreign, or by any insufficiency of domestic consumption.

III.   THE MECHANISM OF TRANSMISSION

Canada's cyclical peak preceded [42] and her early downswing was only slightly less intense [43] than most of those abroad. Judging the following peaks of exports to various areas, the early fall in exports to Britain and Germany may have had a depressing effect on Canadian business:

Germany	July 1928
United Kingdom	November 1928
France	June 1929
United States	November 1929.

But it is primarily the down-turn of vegetable and iron product exports which is of crucial importance since the fall of animal product exports seems to have reflected mainly rising domestic consumption and domestic prices and since the fall in each of the other export categories to any geographical area was more than offset by continued increases to the other areas. [45]   In fact, exports of vegetable products to Britain and Other Countries and exports of iron products to each of the three areas fell before Canada's cyclical down-turn and thus may have contributed to it. Vegetable product exports fell $58 million in one year from their peak in November 1928; this decline was mainly in wheat exports for Britain but partly in those for Other Countries. The major declines of iron product exports between their peak in March--April and the peak of non-farming exports in October were in farm machinery and equipment (mainly to the United States) and vehicles (mainly to Other Countries).

Although the largest absolute fall occurred in vegetable product exports destined for Britain and Other Countries, the decline of wheat exports resulted largely from Canadian policy and thus does not reflect cyclical impulses from abroad. Britain, the United States, and Other Countries contributed to the decline of iron exports. Hence no one geographical area was primarily responsible for the decline in exports.

CHAPTER V

THE DOWNSWING

I. DETERMINANTS

IN THIS CHAPTER the Canadian downswing is found to have been only slightly less intense than the American. All three real determinants as well as the long-term capital account were depressants. Both the fall in exports to the United States and the fall in American capital imports had greater deflationary effects than those in the corresponding transactions with Britain.

The pattern. In 1933 current GNP and national income were only 58 and 51 per cent of their 1929 levels. Real GNP and national income fell slightly less, being 71 and 66 per cent of their 1929 levels. GNP in current prices fell 10.1, 17.8, and 17.4 per cent in the years 1930-2; in real terms it fell 3.9, 12.7, and 8.5 per cent.

The Canadian downswing, 1929-33, was more intense than the British [1] but only slightly less intense than the American [2] and than most of those abroad.

Major determinants. The following table [3] shows that the fall in domestic investment was catastrophic. It fell by 90 per cent compared with 55 for exports and only 34 for consumption. In real terms the disparity in the declines was even greater.

	Peak value	Trough value	Percentage
	(millions of dollars)		fall
Gross domestic investment (inc. inventories)			
in current prices	1,391	146	89.5 (1929-33)
in 1935-9 prices	1,276	134	89.5 (1929-33)
Merchandise exports			
in current prices	1,773	804	54.7 (1928-32)
in 1935-9 prices	1,391	974	30.0 (1928-32)
Domestic consumption			
in current prices	4,393	2,887	34.3 (1929-33)
in 1953-9 prices	3,685	3,055	17.1 (1929-33)

That the acceleration principle offers a partial explanation of the downswing pattern is shown by the table [4] of the percentage changes in real consumption (C) plus exports (E) and in real GNP

Year	Δ (C+E)	Δ GNP
1928-29	+1.3	+0.1
1929-30	-5.7	-3.9
1930-31	-5.8	-12.7
1931-32	-7.1	-8.5
1932-33	-2.2	-7.9
1933-34	+6.8	+11.6

While investment did not behave strictly according to the acceleration principle
during the downswing, still much of it seems to have been closely connected with
the variation of consumption and especially merchandise exports.

Since there was no great difference between the intensity of the Canadian
downswing and those abroad, divergent levels of income were less important in de -
termining the pattern of the trade flow than the types of goods and demand elasticities.

Merchandise exports fell from $1,341 million in 1928 to $495 million in 1932,[5]
imports from $1,272 million in 1929 to $368 million in 1933. The sharp fall of
imports can be attributed mainly to the sharp fall of domestic investment and hence
of the demand for American capital goods, with the fall in demand for luxury imports
and the imposition of higher tariff duties [6] starting in 1930 as contributing factors.
Exports fell less sharply than imports partly because of the magnitude of such exports
as newsprint and wheat, basic components of consumers' goods abroad, production
of which is much more stable than investment, [7] although the weakness of the
British downswing was also important. The sharp depreciation of the Canadian
dollar in September 1931 [8] was only a secondary influence on the export flow . [9]

Merchandise exports do not offer a sufficient criterion by themselves of the
intensity of the fall of Canadian activity, even if allowance is made for the eight-
month lag of GNP behind exports, since they fell least in 1932 while the fall of
GNP in 1932 was almost as sharp as in the previous year. The fall of long-term
capital imports (mainly from the United States)[10] may also have been a depressant
although it was partly the result of the cylical downswing in Canada. [11]

Except for the rise of exports to Britain in 1932, the export flows to the three
geographical areas (United States, United Kingdom, and Other Countries) fell
continuously from 1929 to 1932. The following table [12] shows that the greatest de -
clines were in exports to Other Countries [13] and to the United States:

Exports to	Peak value	Trough value	Percentage fall
	(millions of dollars)		
Britain	$288 (1928)	$139 (1931)	48
United States	519 (1929)	169 (1932)	67
Other Countries	546 (1928)	167 (1933)	69

The fall of real exports to the United States was more significant in contributing
to the Canadian downswing than that of real exports to Britain. The former fell from
a peak of $523 million in 1929 to $244 million in 1932; the latter rose from a trough
of $224 million in 1929 to $225, $259, $302, and $355 million in the next four years.[14]
The most important explanation of this paradoxical rise of real exports to Britain
was that the British downswing was substantially less intense than the Canadian.
Secondly, Canadian exports of building materials (e.g., lumber) to Britain were
increased by the British programme of subsidized public housing. [15] Thus the
Canadian economy was bolstered somewhat throughout the downswing by the rise of
the volume of exports to Great Britain. The fall of the volume of exports to the
United States intensified the Canadian downswing.

It is clear that the primary income effect of the reduced exports to the United

States were greater than those of the reduced exports (at current prices) to Britain.
How strong the comparative secondary income reductions were is not obvious. But
when induced investment is considered, a fairly definite conclusion is obtained.
During the previous upswing the rising export flow to America had led to substantial
domestic investment. Now, with the sharp contraction of these exports, in general
a contraction of related domestic investment occurred. On the other hand, the
investment boom induced by increased exports to Britain was not of such dimensions
and hence its dissolution did not have such widespread depressing effects. Thus
these depressing influences emanating from America contributed more to the
Canadian downswing than those from Britain.

   Conclusion. The American downswing was slightly sharper than the Canadian.
The decline in Canadian exports to the United States, larger than that in exports
to Britain, was a major depressant to the Canadian economy. Long-term capital
imports from the United States also fell more sharply than those from Britain or
Other Countries. The depressing influences from America were much more severe
than those from any other country. As exports fell so did consumption, investment,
and GNP. Investment seemed to be closely geared to consumption expenditure
and particularly merchandise exports throughout the downswing.

II. MECHANISM OF ADJUSTMENT

   The major disturbing force in Canada's balance of payments in the downswing
was the long-term capital account. The major adjusting force was the current
account. Both forces were largely the product of the downswing in Canadian and
foreign business.

   Major independent variable. The yearly correlations between the exchange rate
and the partial balances show that the long-term capital account was the major
account determining the exchange rate in 1930-2. [16] When the monthly partial
balance estimates are correlated with the exchange rate, the long-term capital
account again appears as the "major variable" on the whole in 1931-2 (excluding
the last four months of 1931 when the depreciation of the pound sterling was
primarily responsible for the simultaneous depreciation of the Canadian dollar),
but not in 1930. [17]

   Because of the lack of any close correspondence between the fluctuations of
merchandise imports and the long-term capital balance, the latter does not seem
to have been induced to any great extent by prior fluctuations of merchandise
imports via extensions of book credit. [18] Rather, the fluctuations of long-term
capital flows seem to have resulted largely from the downswing. The fall of the
gross capital inflow from $514 million in 1930 to $322 million in 1931 and $203
million in 1932 was mainly responsible for a similar pattern in the net balance. [19]
New issues of Canadian securities abroad and net direct investment transactions
fell in 1931-2, net sales of outstanding securities in 1931, and insurance transactions
in 1932, as foreign supplies of and the Canadian need for loanable funds fell and as
foreign branch plants in Canada incurred losses and were sold to Canadians. The
rise of the long-term capital account in 1930 largely resulted from the Dominion
Government's borrowing $100 million in New York [20] and a partly fortuitous fall

of retirements and the reversal of net purchases of previously issued securities, the latter reflecting declining Canadian incomes and declining New York stock prices.

Since the major factor in the international accounts was the product of cyclical or independent forces and not of fluctuations of other balance-of-payments items, perhaps this account may be taken as the major independent variable in the balance of payments.

Short-run adjustment processes. [21] In short-run adjustment to the rise in net long-term capital imports in 1930 the Canadian dollar appreciated, the specie premium fell, and net imports of monetary gold totalling $36 million took place. In 1931-2 when net long-term capital imports fell, the Canadian dollar fell, the specie premium rose, [22] and the net monetary gold exports and short-term capital imports [23] totalled $102 million.

In so far as import and export prices were set abroad, they could be expected to fall in 1930 and to rise in 1931-2. Both price indexes did fall in 1930 but continued to fall in the next two years. The 15.8 per cent fall of import prices in 1931-2 despite the depreciation of the Canadian dollar by 13.3 per cent is not surprising since the American price level fell by 25 per cent in the same period. Since the average price of No. 1 Northern Manitoba in London and Liverpool fell by 45.4 per cent, the 29.1 per cent fall of Canadian export prices is hardly surprising.

In so far as export prices might have been determined to some small extent domestically and remained relatively stable, the terms of trade would be expected to turn in Canada's favour in 1930 and conversely in 1931-2. In fact, the terms of trade turned against Canada in 1931 and 1932 -- but also in 1930. The index of the terms of trade fell from 97.9 in 1929 to 92.5, 83.6, and 77.9 in the next three years. But this conformity with simple expectations based on a model with the long-term capital account as the sole variable was assisted greatly by the divergence between the fall of the American price level (32 per cent from 1929 to 1932) and the fall of the prices of Canada's main exports on world markets (No. 1 Northern Manitoba in London and Liverpool fell by 60 per cent from 1929 to 1932).

Nevertheless, most of the expected short-run effects occurred when this pattern of the indpendent external cyclical fluctuation of commodity prices is used as a background. Two exceptions occurred in 1930 when the net movement of short-term capital was nil and the fluctuation of the specie premium was not greater than that of the price level.

Long-run adjustment processes. As expected, a primary contraction of means of payment is revealed in the banking data for 1932 (Table III, column IV). But despite a net monetary gold import of $36 million in 1930 a primary contraction of means of payment is indicated and a primary expansion in 1931 despite a gold export of $33 million. The multiplier-accelerator effect of the primary purchasing power reduction in 1932 also contributed to the decline of national income.

Table III, column III, clearly shows that no secondary expansion of means of payment occurred in any of these years. A fall of total public liabilities as credit contracted was mainly responsible for the rise of the reserve ratio from 7.2 per cent in 1929 to 7.6 in 1930. [24] Most of the 1930 gold import seems to have been used to pay off Finance Act advances. The fall of the reserve ratio to 7.5 per cent in

1931 [25] resulted partly from the external gold drain.[26] It rose to 8.2 per cent in 1932 [27] partly because of the sharp reduction of total public liabilities plus renewed Finance Act borrowing, especially after November when the Canadian Government startled financial circles by forcefully enlarging bank cash reserves by $35 million. Bank loans continued to fall throughout this period despite such occasional improvements in cash reserves. Doubtless the fall in marginal efficiencies of capital resulting from the fall in exports and consumption reduced the demand for bank credit. But there was also pressure by the banks to reduce the credit superstructure.[28] The banks were searching for liquidity but still trying to keep their borrowings under the Finance Act to a minimum. Thus on the whole the banking system appears to have played its equilibrating role in 1931 and 1932 when the sharp reductions in the net long-term capital inflow called for a contraction of bank credit to effect equilibrium in the balance of payments, although the exact extent to which the loan contraction was the result of deliberate policy cannot be determined from the available data.[29] Peculiarly enough, Canada was not strictly on the gold standard at this time. But no price increases or secondary purchasing power effects through bank credit expansion took place in 1930.

TABLE III

Primary and Secondary Contraction of Means of Payment,
Canada, 1930-4[a]

(millions of dollars)

I	II	III	IV
	Primary and		
Year	secondary	Secondary	Primary
	contraction[b]	contraction[c]	contraction[d]
1930	-171	- 92	- 79
1931	- 54	-188	+134
1932	-155	-123	- 32
1933	- 18	-158	+140
1934	+ 30	- 40	+ 70

(a) All data used here are yearly averages of the monthly banking statement in successive issues of C.Y.B.

(b) The net change in the yearly averages of demand and notice deposits in Canada, balances due to Dominion and provincial governments, and notes in circulation.

(c) The net change in the yearly averages of call and short loans in Canada, current loans in Canada, loans to Dominion, provincial, and municipal governments, and overdue debts.

(d) Column II minus column III.

Import prices fell relatively to domestic goods prices in 1930,[30] partly because of the rise in the Canadian dollar, and hence a definite inducement to increase merchandise imports existed. Since the geneeral wholesale price index fluctuated between the indexes of import and of export prices, no definite criterion is available as to the relative behaviour of domestic prices in 1931-2. [31]

The most potent force inducing adjustment to the variations of the long-term capital account balance was the effect of the downswing on the current account. Because of the very high American import content in Canadian domestic investment, the sharp fall in the latter was a major factor [32] in rendering the current account less passive in 1931-2 [33] and thus easing the foreign exchange position. The debit current account balance fell from $337 million in 1930 to $174 and $96 million in 1931 and 1932 while the active long-term capital account balance fell from $373 to $113 and $55 million. Despite the strong cyclical response of the current account no final equilibrium was achieved. The exchange rate also continued to play a direct active adjusting role.

Conclusion. Thus the exchange rate, specie premium, monetary gold and short-term capital movements, international goods prices, and the terms of trade on the whole behaved as expected from the fluctuations of the major independent variable, the long-term capital account, when allowance is made for the independent price fluctuations on world commodity markets. In long-run adjustment a primary contraction of means of payment took place in 1932, a secondart contraction in 1931-2, import prices fell relatively to domestic goods prices in 1930, and, most important, the current account became less passive as a result of the downswing.

For the first and only time in the period studied the orthodox classical mechanism of variations in internal means of payment applied -- but under paper standard conditions rather than gold. Although the contractive policy of the banks may have helped achieve the required curtailment of imports in 1931-2, the major adjusting force was the cyclical variation of the current account. Thus the fluctuations of both the major disturbing factor, the long-term capital account, and of the major equilibrating force, the current account, were largely the direct result of the down-swing. [34]

CHAPTER VI

A MAJOR UP-TURN, 1933

THE REVIVAL of merchandise and gold exports and freight receipts facilitated the Canadian up-turn, which seems to have coincided with most of those abroad. A fall of long-term interest rates may have helped induce a relatively early up-turn of the production of durable producers' goods. Wage reductions at this time on the whole may have hindered recovery because of their harmful effects on consumption expenditure. The most important factor by far was the rise of merchandise exports, which went to no one particular area, and the consequent rise of induced investment.

I. TIMING OF CANADA'S UP-TURN

The medians of the troughs derived from all 71 series, [1] from the 50 seasonally adjusted series, from the 56 volume series, and from the 44 seasonally adjusted volume series came in March 1933. Hence surprisingly close agreement is evidenced by these crude averaging processes. All point to March 1933 as the trough of the Canadian business cycle.

II. CAUSAL FACTORS IN THE UP-TURN

Current account. Three current account credit items may have facilitated the Canadian revival. [2] These were commercial gold exports, which rose fairly steadily after their trough in December 1931, [3] and merchandise exports and freight receipts, both of which rose relatively rapidly after their troughs in December 1932 [4] and February 1933. [5] An examination of the cyclical troughs of each broad commodity

TABLE IV
Sequence of Cyclical Troughs in Canada's
Internal Trade, 1932-33 Up-turn [a]

Year	Month	Series
1931	August	No. of shares traded on Toronto stock exchange.
1932	June	D.B.S. index of business conditions*
		Dominion of Canada long-term bond prices [b]
		Prices of common stock
		Prices of preferred stocks
	July	Coal production*
		Forestry production*
	August	Mineral production*

Table IV (cont' d)

Year	Month	Series
	October	Average daily electrical output*
		Livestock slaughterings * (c)
		Cattle slaughtering *(d)
		Hog slaughterings*
	November	Employment in logging*
		No. of commercial failures, <u>inverse</u> (e)
		Dominion notes in hands of the public*
		Stockyard cattle sales*
		Pneumatic casings produced*
	December	Liabilities of commercial failures, inverse (f)
		Bank debits*
		Production of durable producers' goods*
		No. of shares traded on Montreal stock exchange*(g)
1933	January	Railway carloadings*
		Demand deposits*
		Unemployment in trade unions, <u>inverse</u> (h)
	February	Consumers' goods production*
		Volume of business*
		Industrial production*
		Manufacturing production*
		Iron and steel production*
		Production of foodstuffs*
		Railway passenger miles
		Railway freight ton miles
		Railway operating revenues
		Coke production*
		Wholesale prices
	March	Building permits issued (value)*
		Stockyard calf sales*
		Employment office placements
		Employment office vacancies
		Lead production*
		Newsprint production*(h)
		Production of steel ingots and castings*
	April	Tobacco released for consumption*
		No. of strikes (i)
		Retail sales* (i)
		Distribution*
	May	Pig iron production* (j)
		Employment in manufacturing*
		Employment in mining*

Table IV (cont'd)

Year	Month	Series
1933	May	Employment in trade*
		Employment in services
		Construction*
	June	Employment in all industries*
		Cost of living (h)
	July	Employment in construction and maintenance*
	November	Sheep Slaughterings *(k)
	December	Employment in transportation*
		New bond issues
		Stockyard hog sales*
		Livestock marketings*
		Wheat receipts*
		Grain marketings*
		Agricultural marketings*
		Production of boots and shoes*
1934	March	Employment in communications
	April	Cold storage holdings*
	May	Employment office applications, inverse (l)
	July	Current bank loans *
	November	Automobile production* (m)
	December	No. of employees on strike
		No. of days lost in strikes

* Seasonally adjusted series.
(a) See Appendix D for statistical sources. All production series are physical volume series unless otherwise stated.
(b) Lower value 5 months previous.
(c) Lower values 22, 23, and 24 months previous.
(d) Lower value 12 months previous.
(e) Lower inverted value 10 months previous.
(f) Lower inverted value 12 months previous.
(g) Lower values 10, 11, and 12 months earlier.
(h) Same value in previous month.
(i) Same value 2 months previous.
(j) Same value in 2 previous months.
(k) Lower value in April 1930.
(l) Lower inverted value in October 1931.
(m) Lower values 36 and 37 months previous.

export category reveals that all but two had turning-points in or before February 1933.[6] Moreover, the other two troughs came in the March-April period where the fiscal-year-end distortion of customs returns renders an exact determination impossible. Since

these two troughs may well have come in March 1933 the curious pattern arises of
revivals in each export category either simultaneous with or preceding the Canadian
business cycle revival. This rise of merchandise exports must be recognized as a very
important contribution to the Canadian up-turn.

Long-term capital account. The gross capital inflow rose merely from $443
million in 1933 to $459 million in 1934; and the inflow actually fell from $154 to
$138 million when the gross sales of outstanding securities are deleted. The gross
capital outflow rose from $484 million in 1933 to $550 million in 1934; but the outflow remained relatively stable at $246 and $238 million when purchases of outstanding
securities are ignored. According to our monthly estimates the net balance of this
account fell fairly regularly from an inflow of $67 million in December 1929 to a
net outflow of $67 million in November 1933. Moreover, when the seasonal pattern
is considered the net long-term capital import about the time of the up-turn seems
quite small. Thus long-term capital imports cannot have been an important factor
in the 1933 up-turn.

Balancing account. While the loss of international reserves in the first quarter
of 1933 was relatively small compared with the usual seasonal pattern, [7] no great
transfer of purchasing power from abroad appears to have occurred. It is true that,
on the whole, the current account was the dominant variable in the balance of
payments. [8] But despite the improvement of this account, the external value of the
Canadian dollar fell relatively steadily. The price of the New York dollar in Canada
rose from $1.143352 in January 1933 to $1.197484 in February and remained relatively
stable at $1.19731 in March. Thus the smallness of the reduction of Canada's
international reserves did not mean that increased purchasing power was being obtained
from abroad, and hence the expansionary forces so far discovered in the balance of
payments must be regarded as having been somewhat less potent than they at first
seemed. Still the change in expectations and the induced investment effects of the
early rise of merchandise exports appear to have been major stimuli.

Monetary policy. Despite the abnormally small loss of international reserves in
the first quarter of 1933 the commercial banks seem to have maintained their
traditional policy of relatively stable rates on loans and savings deposits until May 1,
1933. [9] The reluctance of the banks to borrow under the Finance Act was increased
when the rate on these advances was raised from 3 to 3 1/2 per cent in May 1932. [10]

To the surprise of Canadian financial circles the Government diverged from its
hitherto orthodox policy in November 1932 by (i) a forced sale to the chartered banks
of $35 million two-year Treasury Bills and (ii) the imposition on the banks of an
obligation to borrow Dominion notes using these Bills as collateral. The Dominion
note issue under the Finance Act and the monetary base were thus enlarged by $35
million at a time when the banks were trying to keep their borrowings as low as
possible for fear of being considered in an unsound position. This implementation of
the Ottawa Agreement [11] rendered unnecessary deflationary policies by the banks
aimed at improving their reserve positions. [12] But the credit superstructure was not
enlarged to any significant extent. The seasonally adjusted indexes of current and
of call loans in Canada continued to fall. [13] As in the two previous turning-points
examined, both call and current loans were relatively late in reflecting the movements
of the Canadian business cycle.

Thus the enforced enlargement of bank reserves in November 1932 did not contribute greatly to the Canadian revival.[14] It may have contributed slightly to the lowering of the long-term rate of interest through increased bank security purchases[15] and may have contributed to the increase in the quantity of money in the hands of the public.[16] The point here, however, is that banking action was not of great importance in stimulating the Canadian up-turn itself although it may have contributed later to the upswing. Nor did the relative improvement of the balancing account contribute to the up-turn by means of banking action.

Consumption. The percentage of real GNP consumed fell from 82.5 in 1932 to 81.3 in 1933 and 76.3 in 1934;[17] that of disposable income was 103.6, 104.1, and 99.6. Thus the up-turn itself was not accompanied by any spectacular increase in consumption.[18] Moreover, the rise of the rate of growth of consumption, from minus 3.1 in 1933 to plus 5.1 per cent in 1934, seems too gradual to have been a major recuperating force, especially when compared with the 14.7 per cent rise in 1922. In addition, one trough of the seasonally adjusted series on retail sales comes a month before the Canadian cyclical trough, the other a month after the Canadian cyclical trough. In so far as most sectors of Canadian business experienced revivals (by March) before the lasting revival of domestic consumption (after April),[19] the rise of the latter was a factor contributing to the upswing but not to the up-turn.[20] The rise of exports by 0.8 per cent in 1933 and 12.1 per cent in 1934, contributed more to the rise of induced investment[21] than did consumption. One must look elsewhere than in the field of consumption for an explanation of this up-turn.

Yield. While yield fell from an index of 108.7 in 1932 to 97.7 in 1933,[22] the price of preferred stocks rose slightly from 52.8 to 55.9 and common stock prices from 55.6 to 68.6. Yield on corporation bonds fell .11 percentage points in 1933 compared with .41 in pure yield. Thus the fall of pure yield appears to have been the dominant feature of the security and stock markets.[23] The change of risk premium seems to have been important only in the market for ordinary shares.

But despite the sharpness of the fall in yield, total issues of new bonds rose only gradually from $468 million in 1932 to $529 million in 1933 and $584 million in 1934. Construction and gross domestic investment rose by 23 and 139 per cent in 1934,[24] but the volume of construction did not rise until after May 1933 and that of automobile production until after November 1934. Only the volume of production of durable producers' goods rose relatively early, after December 1932, before the cyclical up-turn of general business. Thus while the fall of yield may have contributed substantially to the early upswing, from the statistics available only its possible stimulation of the production of durable producers' goods may have contributed to the up-turn itself.[25] Obviously we must look elsewhere for powerful contributing stimuli.[36]

Wage rates. The general weighted average of wage rates fell from a peak index of 197.1 in 1930 to 189.1, 177.7, and a trough of 168.3 in the next three years. Mainly because of decreased wage rates, wage-cost per unit in manufacturing industries fell slightly from a peak of 114.2 in 1932 to 97.4 in 1933.[27] But the wage reductions in the durable goods industries did not provoke any strong expansionary tendencies.[28] First, on the whole, the decline of union wage rates in the heavier industries was not particularly sharp. Only the fall in the building trades exceeded

that of the general weighted average.[29]   Secondly, the reductions did not take place
in a short period but continued throughout the downswing and in some cases in the
early upswing. Thirdly, it does not seem probable that expectations in the construction industry were very inelastic. [30] On the whole, these wage reductions at the
time of the up-turn were probably more of a hindrance to recovery because of their
reaction on consumption than a help because they reduced costs for firms.

Innovations. The increase of industrial productivity[31] was relatively low in 1933,
0.2 per cent, compared with 6.8 in 1922. Lack of technical progress is also evidenced
by the relative fortunes of different industries. Of the eleven sectors of the economy
whose growth has been examined previously, only six showed any gain from 1929 to
1937 [32] according to the annual data. It is true that some of the industries which
experienced fundamental innovations and the most rapid advances in the 20's continued to expand in the 30's; but these increases were small. [38] In the 20's different
industries exhibited sharply varying fortunes; in the 30's all groups tended to concentrate closer to the average. Thus the innovations largely responsible for the expansion of th 20's were no longer potent accelerators and no major new ones came
upon the scene. [34]

Summary. The most important stimulus to the Canadian up-turn seems to have
come from abroad. Total exports and most (if not all) of the broad export categories
rose before the turning-point of business in general. No longer was the revival of
one or two exports sufficient to engender a revival of Canadian business as a whole by
inducing extensive domestic investment. No longer were domestic expectations so
favourable that one or two potentially auspicious developments on the international
front induced general optimism and general recovery. Almost all export categories
had to experience an expansion of activity before the economy recuperated, although
the recovery in certain sectors, especially the Prairies, was very slight. Canada's
business cycle appeared to be more dependent directly on foreign demand than at
any other time of the period under study, partly because excess capacity prevailed in
most of the major export fields.

Induced investment and the early revival of commercial gold exports and freight
receipts also seem to have been stimulating influences. To some extent a fall of yield
may have facilitated the up-turn by inducing an early recovery in the production of
durable producers' goods but this was not a key determinant.

III. MECHANISM OF CYCLICAL TRANSMISSION

Canada's cyclical trough seems to have coincided with [35] and her early upswing
to have been as intense as [36] most of those abroad. Her merchandise export flows
to Britain, France, the United States, Germany, and Other Countries [37] rose before
Canada's cyclical up-turn and hence may have facilitated it.

When the separate categories of exports to each of the three main geographical
areas are examined, almost all of them reveal cyclical troughs in or before April
1933. [38] Thus no one country or geographical area was primarily responsible for
the early rise of Canadian exports. Nevertheless exports to Britain and America were
more important in stimulating the Canadian up-turn than those to Other Countries.[39]
All three areas contributed to the rise of freight receipts in 1933-4 although American
and British receipts were more important than those from Other Countries. [40] It seems

that most commercial gold exports went to the principal market for the world's gold, the United States. [41] Thus no one country was responsible for the rise of these three credits items in Canada's balance of payments. Nor does any criterion of the net stimulating effect of each of the various credit flows present itself. As in the two previous turning-points examined, several countries contributed to the crucial influences on Canada's international activity through the international accounts.

CHAPTER VII

CONSISTENCY OF HYPOTHESES

I. RELATIVE TIMING AND STRENGTH

IT WAS FOUND above that, contrary to a common belief, the turning-points of a
country highly dependent upon international trade need not lag behind those of more
highly industrialized countries or of its major export markets, [1] although when this
does occur the expansion is not likely to proceed very rapidly.

A number of different factors might be responsible for such a phenomenon. First,
if the minor country specializes in the production of one product such as wool (say)
and if the textile industry in the highly industrialized major countries tends to slump
relatively early, [2] the down-turn of general activity in the minor country might well
precede that in the major countries. This sequence might be especially applicable
where the relevant industry in the major countries is not predominant. Secondly, a
down-turn of activity might precede in such a minor country if expectations are
unfavourable, for example because a price decline is expected. These unfavourable
expectations may lead to a substantial decline in the volume of domestic investment
without any prior decrease in exports. Thirdly, domestic "real" forces in the minor
country may effect a turning-point of general activity without any depressing effect
emanating from the export markets. Inelastic factor supply, for instance, may mean
the disappointment of investment plans and contribute to a relatively early down-turn.
Thus a minor country such as Canada can easily get into difficulties by herself but
that need not mean that other countries would be influenced greatly by these
difficulties.

Thus the conclusion that cyclical turning-points may occasionally precede in
minor countries is not at all unreasonable. It must be pointed out, however, that
no one pattern need prevail for any one country. Moreover, the factors responsible
for the turning-points need never be the same; domestic forces might predominate in
one instance, international forces in the next.

Similarly, no one pattern need prevail regarding the relative amplitude of cyclical
fluctuations in various countries, whether economically "young" or "old." Either
type may expand more rapidly than the other for a short time and then expand less
rapidly. Thus, while the level of exports might be rising, induced domestic investment might be relatively low until exports had risen to a relatively high level.
But if domestic investment rises rapidly with the widespread application of innovations
and if the distribution of income encourages a steady and high level of consumption
expenditure, the consequent expansion in the minor country might well exceed in
violence expansions elsewhere. If the function relating disposable income to GNP
shifts in a negative direction, the rate of expansion of general activity might be
slow because of the partial depression--absolute or relative--of the consumers'
goods industries. In time no doubt the economy could achieve a high level of
activity despite such a change in the composition of national product; but during the

transition much distress might well result.

II. MECHANISMS OF TRANSMISSION AND ADJUSTMENT

Monetary Theories

Cyclical impulses. It was seen in the previous chapters that substantial variations occurred in Canadian merchandise stocks during the 1920's despite the fact that the rates at which advances could be obtained from the commercial banks remained relatively stable. This fact makes one suspicious of the supposed all-powerful effect of bank rates on inventory holdings.[3] Hawtrey has stated that the prospects of price fluctuations are likely to be more important than interest rate fluctuations as regards agricultural products and has qualified this theory so as to pertain to manufactured goods only.[4] But again both the volume and the value data on manufactured goods stocks reveal substantial fluctuations despite relative stability of short-term rates.[5]

Such tests are pointless, however, according to Hawtrey, since consumers' demand will reduce stocks as rapidly as lowered interest rates induce increases.[6] Moreover, is such increases are impossible because the relevant productive factors are already fully employed, wholesale prices will rise as a result of the merchants' increased demand for stocks and hence incomes and consumption expenditure will also rise. " If, as is likely, retail prices lag behind wholesale prices, consumption will exceed production, stocks will be diminished." [27] Hence it is the paradox of credit regulation that an opposing tendency is set up which may just counterbalance or more than offset the original tendency induced by the change of interest rates.

Nevertheless, at least one empirical test appears possible. Effective changes of the rates on bank advances or in credit policies would be expected near the turning-points of the business cycle. But the Canadian banking system seems to have been, on the whole, a passive rather than an active factor as regards cyclical variations of Canadian business. As the empirical chapters evidenced, neither direct (i.e., credit rationing) nor interest rate policies seem to have caused the turning-point of general activity in any of the cases examined.

Perhaps this theory of the trade cycle has been found inapplicable because Canada was not a "great financial centre." According to Hawtrey, a country which is not a "great financial centre" is less susceptible to variations of credit since a greater proportion of its internal short-term indebtedness is due from producers, with a relatively large fraction of its export and import trade usually being financed in foreign centres.[8] Since producers are generally less dependent upon others for working capital than are dealers,[9] centres financing most of the dealers of their own national unit would presumably be better able to influence the level of business activity than centres dependent upon foreign financing. Conversely, fluctuations of the volume of credit in great financial centres would tend to affect and determine the volume of activity not only at home but also abroad.[10] In this fashion, according to Hawtrey, changes in the bank rate in London affected other nations quickly in the period prior to World War I. "The world credit movements were initiated in London, and tended to spread to all other countries without further action." [11] Hence fluctuations of real activity in the great financial centres would be expected to precede and determine fluctuations in such lesser centres as Canada. [12] Perhaps it would be unreasonable, therefore, to expect the volume of credit inside Canada itself to be the prime initiator of cyclical turnings.

Still, if this be the case, presumably cyclical fluctuations in Canada must have followed the fluctuations of real activity in the relevant great financial centres. But since the major turning-points of the Canadian business cycle appear to have preceded most of those abroad in two major cases and to have coincided in the other case, no evidence substantiating the Hawtrey theory appears. It seems reasonable to conclude that the turning-points of the Canadian business cycle were not effected primarily either by domestic or by foreign variations of the volume of credit.

Mechanism of Adjustment. Hawtrey's theory that, as a business expansion proceeds at a faster pace in one country than another, monetary gold will flow from the former to the latter, appears to be substantiated by the Canadian experience throughout the 1921-9 upswing as a whole. In 1921-5, when Canada's expansion was relatively slow, monetary gold imports and short-term capital exports generally occurred. In 1926-9 when Canada's expansion was relatively intense, monetary gold exports and short-term capital imports prevailed.

But how can this partial substantiation of Hawtrey's thesis be reconciled with its apparent failure in the case of Britain before World War I? Hawtrey's model, held as the standard view of the cyclical behaviour of the balance of payments, has been put into serious doubt by Beach's research on British pre-1914 experience. [14] Beach found that British gold imports rose during business prosperity and gold exports during the depression. [15] With such a finding, an application of the conclusion arrived at in our previous chapters would make one suspect that the amplitude of the British business cycle might have been somewhat smaller than those in the rest of the world. But Beach rejects this explanation of the behaviour of the British balance of payments. [16] His first objection is that "the adjustment through the price mechanism must be very prompt. International trade must respond quickly to changes in the general level of prices. Over periods so short as the business cycle it is not certain that these adjustments will be made rapidly enough for gold movements to play the role assigned to them." [17] His objection is perfectly valid in so far as the price-specie-flow mechanism is concerned and is reinforced by the study of this Canadian experience. One cannot place any great degree of dependence upon the "classical" mechanism for adjustment to gaps in the balance of payments if the present results are acceptable. Flows of international reserves were not accompanied by any equilibrating bank credit variations except in part of the downswing. [18]

But Beach's criticism can hardly apply to the shifts-in-demand-schedules mechanism [19] which seems to have been one of the more notable mechanisms securing adjustment in this Canadian instance. Both primary income and secondary (multiplier-accelerator) income effects are extremely important in achieving adjustment to balance-of-payments gaps because of their inherent automatic nature. Another automatic mechanism tending to alter the level of purchasing power is the change in demand for credit resulting from altered marginal efficiencies of capital. [20] Moreover, all of these automatic mechanisms altering the level of purchasing power seem to have been operating at least to some extent at various phases of the Canadian case studied. In this very pertinent regard, therefore, Beach's objection is hardly valid. [21] Once the classical merchandise model is resuscitated with these mechanisms, it cannot be dismissed so easily. As cyclical expansion abroad proceeded at a faster pace,[22] English exports would rise faster than English imports with a resulting more active or less passive balance of trade. Moreover, gold imports would be expected during the boom in so far as the balance of trade was the major independent variable of England's international accounts. [23]

Beach's second objection to the modified classical position is that "the fluctua- tions in foreign loans should permit relatively higher price levels in borrowing countries during ... prosperity .. and ... greater fall in these levels during depres- sion, as compared with creditor nations," if the classical model is correct. The "chief defect with the classical explanation is that lower price levels in prosperity in the older' nations ... would lead to specie imports if price levels govern the situation, but would be consistent with specie exports if there was a larger volume of international lending...."[24] In so far as the amplitude of price fluctuations in borrowing countries may have been substantially greater than in England, the possibility arises of a relatively large volume of merchandise exports from England in prosperity and hence perhaps of gold imports.

Beach's objection appears a pertinent qualification but hardly a ground for re- jecting the classical theory. Hawtrey noted that the export of capital from the old countries to the new correlated positively with the fluctuations of the business cycle in the lending countries. [25] Moreover, he noted not only the tendency for the amplitude of credit variations to be greater in the borrowing than in the lending countries but also the direction of the gold movements in such a model with the long- term capital account as the major independent variable. [26] What Beach has done is to weld the two Hawtrey models into one, something which Hawtrey himself did not attempt to do. Thus if the increment of foreign loans exceeded that of merchandise exports in prosperity, gold exports from the creditor would result. [27] It would be a question of fact in each particular case whether the relative changes of the price levels [28] -- induced in part, doubtless, by the foreign lending--led to fluctuations in international trade which swamped the flow of external lending. The direction of the gold flow would depend, then, upon which factor was quantitatively more significant. Focusing his attention solely on Hawtrey's merchandise model, Beach says it is untenable a priori because it ignores these difficulties concerning capital movements.

On the basis of these two objections, Beach dismisses the classical hypothesis as not dependable a priori and concludes that other factors must explain the cyclical behaviour he discovered. It seems clear, however, (i) that his first objection is un- convincing and unsatisfactory because it ignore the vital and speedy role of the shifts-in-demand mechanism and (ii) that his second objection is merely a qualification of one of Hawtrey's models. Certainly this latter qualification is valid but it is not a ground for rejecting completely the whole schema. With full provision for the shifts- in-demand mechanism, Beach's combined model of the classical position takes on a new potency and appears basic to the understanding of such occurrences as were analysed in the previous chapters. According to the diagnosis of this Canadian case, important elements of both the current and the long-term capital accounts seem to

have fluctuated in a cyclical fashion but usually one of them could be selected as
being quantitatively more significant. [29]

Beach favours his alternative hypothesis [30] which turns on the fact that both
England and the United States had relatively inelastic supplies of credit and both
used a standard money coin for a large proportion of public cash transactions. The
internal drain of coin into circulation in prosperity was more responsible for depleting
bank reserves than was the increase of bank credit. "The pressure upon bank reserves
led to increased discount rates in the money markets, and the flow of short-term
capital, induced as a consequence, may well have been the dominating factor determining the gold flows over cyclical periods." [31]

Can Beach's theory explain Canadian short-term capital movements? Occasionally
short-term capital movements were quite large and may have been the dominant item
in Canada's international accounts. But those which have been estimated on either
a monthly or an annual basis do not seem to have been the prime determinant of
gold flows. [32]   As seen in the previous chapters, short-term capital movements
definitely behaved in an equilibrating rather than in a disturbing fashion. The
annual estimates of the net changes in bank balances abroad reveal only few exceptions
from equilibrating behaviour. [33]   In addition the net sales of outstanding securities
generally showed greater evidence of equilibrating behaviour. [34] Thus Beach's
hypothesis can hardly apply to this Canadian experience. [35]

Hence Hawtrey's balance of payments models have been found relevant throughout - but only when they are combined into one and when an attempt has been made
to ascertain the major factor in each case. [36]

Monetary Undersaving

Domestic sphere. On the whole Hayek's theory does not explain the Canadian
business cycle. In the 1921 up-turn, one cannot be certain whether the equilibrium
rate of interest rose above the market rate if the former is identified with the expected
rate of profit and the latter with the rate on bank advances. [37] But even if it did, both
current bank loans and the total of loans plus security holdings actually fell rather than
increased. Even if allowance is made for the falling price level by dividing these
series by the wholesale price index, the resulting "real" series remained relatively
stable from 1921 to 1923. No forced savings through increased bank credit occurred.

Since the 1921 up-turn and early upswing occurred without any strong assistance
from the banks one might expect that this theory would not apply to the subsequent
down-turn. It is true that the volume of bank credit grew at a remarkably fast pace
in the last few years of the upswing and that the 1929 price increases may evidence
some degree of forced saving. But no "evidence" of inflationary tendencies appeared
until slightly after the down-turn of activity in general. Nor was the 1933 up-turn
brought about by increased bank lending.

International extension.   The increased volume of means of payment in Canada
in the last few years of the upswing was not created by any inflow of international
reserves. Rather, large monetary gold exports and short-term capital imports occurred,
1926-9, with bank reserves replenished by Finance Act borrowing. Although a relatively
large inflow of reserves might lead, under a fractional reserve system, to a more than
proportionate increase of bank credit and perhaps a disproportionate increase of the

capital structure as Hayek suggests, [38] no such sequence occurred in this Canadian case.

Nor was the Canadian down-turn associated with any cessation of long-term capital imports, although it is true that long-term capital imports from the United States facilitated the 1921 up-turn and also to some extent the early upswing. Thus while the cessation of American long-term capital exports may well have been partly responsible for the relatively early German collapse, the same sequence is not applicable to Canada.

Nurkse's claim [39] that the flow of international funds was reversed in 1928-9 is substantiated by Canadian experience but only in exactly the reverse sequence. In 1928 a net long-term capital export of $104 million occurred; in 1929 a net import of $186 million.

Nor was the Canadian down-turn itself caused by the American collapse. [40] It may well be, however, that Canada was in an unusual position in this regard. [41]

Non-Monetary Undersaving.

Domestic sphere. The theory of real undersaving appears to be only slightly more applicable to this Canadian cycle than that of the monetary variety. Despite the occasionally close connection between thrift and the long-term rate of interest, the latter does not appear to have been of predominant importance in any of the turning-points. [42] While the long-term interest rate fell both in 1921 and in 1933 when the percentage of GNP saved rose, this fall was only of minor importance in 1921 and was even less potent in 1933 when it stimulated few, if any, investment categories. Although the percentage of GNP saved fell (because of a shift of the consumption function) in 1929 and yield rose, no evidence of a significant capital shortage was found.

But other variables stressed by undersaving theorists were important occasionally in certain sectors of the economy at least. Thus the sharp money wage-rate cuts in the durable goods industries in 1921 may have provided some net expansionary stimulus [43] -- especially since no unfavourable repercussion on consumption expenditure took place in 1921-2. Similarly, the sharp wage increases in the construction industry may have been partly responsible for its relatively early down-turn in 1929, although the gradualness of wage increases throughout the economy as a whole probably was an important factor in maintaining consumption expenditure. The interesting conclusion emerges that seemingly divergent theories might be applicable as explanations of the same turning-point. Thus, on the one hand, some critical sectors of the economy might suffer from inelastic factor supply and reach a ceiling in their production with a consequent decline in induced investment in industries subsidiary to them. On the other hand, other sectors of the economy might suffer at the same time from a decline of exports or excessive capital investment in relation to sales opportunities. On the whole the Keynesian thesis that the profitableness of investment opportunities varies primarily for reasons not connected with changes in cost items appears to be more relevant to the turning-points studied. But the contrary theory is not to be dismissed since on occasion it seems to help explain certain aspects of the turning-point of general activity.

External sphere. (i) It was found in the empirical chapters that long-term capital imports fell in the post-war and 1931-2 depressions. On the whole large

capital imports occurred in 1921 and in the first half of the upswing; in the latter
half either the net long-term capital imports were relatively small or capital exports
occurred The 1929 down-turn itself, however, cannot be explained in terms of
curtailment of capital imports since renewed net capital imports began that year and
increased in 1930. Moreover, the 1933 up-turn was not assisted by any net long-
term capital import. [44] Thus the pattern of the 1921 up-turn, the early upswing, and
the 1931-2 downswing may be explained in part by the availability of foreign savings.
Still since the flow of long-term capital did not help bring about two of the major
turning-points examined, it is definitely impossible to cite the varying rate of
capital import as the sole "efficient cause" of the level of Canadian activity as Wood
has contended for Australia. [45]

On the whole the long-term capital movements seem to have been largely
determined by, rather than to have been a major determinant of, the business cycle.
As was seen in the sections on mechanism of adjustment, important elements of the
long-term capital account often oscillated in a cyclical fashion. Thus in 1922,
when Canada's early upswing was relatively rapid, rather large capital imports
occurred. In the next three years, when expansion was generally less intense than
most of those abroad, these imports steadily declined and then the capital flow was
reversed. In 1931-2 as the profitability of investment in Canada declined and as
world depression (involving increased risk and lowered incomes) decreased the
available foreign savings, the net import balance of the long-term capital account
declined steadily. In 1933, again, an export balance appeared largely because of
the great number of maturities and redemptions. Aside from the 1930 discrepancy,
which arose largely from government borrowing, [46] the latter half of the upswing
is the main exception to a cyclical explanation of Canada's net long-term capital
account movements. In 1926 and 1929 fairly long-term capital imports occurred
as Canada's upswing was generally more intense than those abroad, but not in 1927-8
These few exceptions do not invalidate the general conclusion that, on the whole,
the long-term capital account balance appears to have fluctuated in a cyclical
pattern and often in response to the relative strength of cyclical fluctuations at home
and abroad. [47]

(ii) Since important long-term capital items fluctuated in a cyclical pattern,
Angell's scepticism [48] is hardly justified. Compilations given in Table V show that
the flotations of Canada's new corporate bond issues on the American market were
concentrated mainly in 1926-9 when Canada's upswing was relatively intense--
as were stock flotations also, contrary to Angell's thesis. Moreover, the peak flotations
of both corporate bonds and stocks [49] came when Canada's upswing was relatively
sharp. New government bond issues did not fit any simple cyclical hypothesis.

The fact of the matter is that the prospect of rising profits or capital gains
induces foreign investment in shares at the same time that relatively low prices induce investment in fixed-income securities. [50] In addition to this rational behaviour, the cyclical oscillations of psychological extremes, the excessive optimism
of prosperity and the excessive pessimism of depression, tend to reinforce this
pattern. If the cyclical expansion and hence the expected rate of profit are substantially greater in country A than in B, A would tend to have capital imports; and

conversely if the speed of the downswing was more intense in A. The relative strength of cyclical fluctuations, rather than the type of security involved as Angell contends, appears to be the dominant factor determining the direction of the capital movement.

TABLE V

Canadian Financing in the United States
New Issues, 1922-35 (a)

(millions of American dollars)

Year	Government bonds	Corporate long-term bonds & notes	Corporate common stocks	Corporate preferred stocks	Corporate short-term financing
1922	94.0	25.8	...	3.5	11.2
1923	26.3	29.8	...	...	...
1924	132.4	74.1	...	...	23.8
1925	49.2	69.3	...	5.3	20.0
1926	60.8	135.4	.4	4.0	1.3
1927	89.3	194.4	2.0	16.8	2.0
1928	35.0	148.5	8.6	26.1	.3
1929	52.3	285.6	18.2	10.4	...
1930	130.8	214.0	18.6	13.0	5.7
1931	40.9	140.0	...	...	...
1932	26.0	...	...	...	...
1933	...	...	.1	...	...
1934	...	...	...	...	...
1935	...	...	...	...	...

(a)　Compiled from the Chronical (New York) and the Commercial and Financial Chronicle. An attempt has been made to take the latest revised figures. When only the current figures were available, the sum of the monthly totals has been taken instead of the often slightly divergent yearly total.

In this manner perhaps the positive correlation between pre-1914 British capital exports and the British business cycle [51] might be explained by the fact that cyclical oscillations abroad had a greater amplitude than the British. [52] In so far as American capital exports seem to have fluctuated inversely with the level of activity during the 1920's, [53] one explanation may be that the amplitude of the American business cycle was greater than those abroad. [54] The fact that no consistent correlation appears in the case of France [55] perhaps may be explained by the possibility of different rates of cyclical expansion in France and abroad, as White himself has mentioned. [56]

The general conclusion from this Canadian experience does not conflict with that of Viner since he recognized the possibility of such a correlation if the "capital-exporting countries are typically countries whose business cycles always precede or lag after world cycles. " [57] What is important here, however, is that the correlation need not be consistent throughout for any one country since its relative rate of expansion or recession will tend to vary and hence also the correlation with long-term capital movements. [58] To judge by this Canadian experience, one is not justified in expecting any one country to maintain a consistently sharper rate of cyclical movement but rather in expecting it to be now a bit ahead and then a bit behind the movement of activity abroad. With a time-lag, the flow of long-term capital would tend to conform to the relative rates of cumulative expansion or contraction in the absence of great political or institutional barriers. [59]

But this statement must be qualified. First, government borrowing may not conform closely with the cyclical industrial pattern and may even have an anti-cyclical pattern, for depression difficulties may induce larger borrowing. Secondly, to some extent the bunching of redemptions is the result of historical cycles and not of current cyclical conditions. Thirdly, on occasion the relative creditor-debtor status of the country may be responsible for divergences. Thus with a greater amplitude of the trade cycle in the debtor country capital exports to creditors might prove difficult because of a dearth of savings. But even here the necessity of meeting repayments and maturities might sustain the general pattern. Fourthly, if the mobility of capital be less than perfect, complications will of course arise. For example, the rapid growth of an adequate domestic capital market in a debtor country which has formerly taken the initiative in offering securities abroad, plus easy bank credit, might induce a switch to the domestic market; or inadequate knowledge and undeveloped institutions might prevent the creditor nations from infiltrating immediately to any great extent into the more rapidly expanding debtor country. Fifthly, even if the upswing be more intense in country A, net capital exports may prevail because the investors are seeking capital appreciation rather than high yield or are seeking safer investments than can be procured at home. Under these circumstances the supply of capital is not homogeneous and substantial imports and exports may both develop at the same time. Sixthly, even if cyclical oscillations had the same amplitude and timing in both creditor and debtor countries, (a) the cyclical fluctuations in the availability of savings resulting from the cyclical fluctuations of income and (b) the cyclical fluctuations in the margin of irrationality of the creditor country's investors would tend to bring about a somewhat similar pattern in the flow of capital to the debtor countries. [60]

To some extent these qualifications may be illustrated by the behaviour of Canada's balance of payments. The independent behaviour of government borrowing appears to have been mainly responsible for the 1930 divergence from the general pattern and to have contributed to that of 1928. The random nature of maturities and redemptions [61] accounted in part for the 1928 divergence and for the tendency toward a net capital export in 1931-3. New domestic capital supplies and relatively imperfect arrangements for creditors to take much initiative also helps explain the 1927-8 divergence. As internal corporation and other savings rose swiftly, there was little incentive to incur foreign debt. Another important element explaining the 1927 divergence would be the type of capital mainly available [63] in Canada. The large import of outstanding securities in 1927 seems to have been made for such reasons as security, diversification of holdings, and capital appreciation in New York, with the relative speed of the upswing or relative yields not considered important. Moreover the dearth of savings [64] and increased pessimism prevailing in depression may help explain the behaviour of Canada's long-term capital account during the 1929-33 downswing when Canadian contractive forces were only slightly less intense than those abroad.

(iii) Since long-term capital movements are not likely to offset each other but rather to fluctuate in response to cyclical forces, they may well strengthen the receiving country's expansion as Robbins and Nurkse have pointed out. In so far as they originate in inflationary financing in the creditor country, serious distortions of the capital structure in the capital-importing country may result whenever the source of savings gives out. But even if they are based entirely upon voluntary savings, the consequences of a sudden reversal must assuredly bring difficulties for the borrowing country. [65]

(iv) Mechanism of adjustment. Throughout 1921-33 the long-term capital and current account balances were kept in rough equality mainly by their common dependence upon the relative strength of cyclical fluctuations. When business expansion abroad was faster than Canada's in the first half of the upswing, on the whole Canada's current account grew progressively more active as merchandise exports rose and her long-term capital account became progressively less active or more passive as capital imports fell off. When Canada's expansion proceeded at a faster pace than most of those abroad, the current account became steadily less active or more passive as merchandise imports rose and, except for 1927-8, the long-term capital account became progressively more active. During the downswing the long-term capital account generally grew less active as foreign supplies of savings dwindled and maturities and redemptions remained at a relatively high level, while the current account became steadily less passive because of the luxury and investment nature of Canada's imports. Aside from 1930-2 when the equilibrating tendencies of the long-term capital and current accounts did not result mainly from the relative strength of the downswing, relative cyclical conditions appear to have been primarily responsible for the equilibrating tendencies in the long-term capital and current accounts.

Taussig was troubled in his research by the fact that many adjustments seemed to have been made more quickly and with considerably less friction than this theory would lead one to expect. [66] In the light of this Canadian experience, perhaps it is not unreasonable to conclude that the response of the balance of payments to relative cyclical conditions at home and abroad may provide at least part of the explanation of this uncanny tendency of the current and long-term capital accounts to balance. [67]

Other mechanism of adjustment theories are still vitally important, since the forces they emphasize may operate to close the remaining gap in the balance of payments. In this role, monetary gold and short-term capital flows are of crucial significance. While the short-term capital flow was larger than that of monetary gold, both contributed to the adjustment; both seemed to be mainly dependent upon the state of the balance of payments rather than unrelated autonomous variables.

Moreover, automatic purchasing power variations seemed to have existed throughout
most of the period, but seldom price or secondary purchasing power changes dependent
upon bank loans. Under certain circumstances, these other theories may be the sole
hypotheses relevant; but if one is to judge from this Canadian experience, the influence
of the relative strength of the business cycle may be more important. [68]

Underconsumption

The thesis that the villain of the piece is insufficient domestic consumption is on the
whole inapplicable, although negative shifts in the function relating consumption to personal income did slow down the upswings in 1923-4 and in 1934. [69] No significant correlation was found between investment and the marginal propensity to consume. Nor
could the 1929 down-turn be attributed to a declining marginal propensity to consume. [70]

The acceleration principle occasionally helps to explain the level of Canadian
activity. It does not, of course, provide a complete explanation of the behaviour of
investment even when the percentage change of consumption plus merchandise exports is taken as the basis of acceleration and when allowance is made for excess
capacity at low levels of output, [71] partly because of the importance of replacement
and public investment and the widespread commercial application of innovations.
Although large sectors of investment were autonomous [72] rather than induced --
as is indicated by the lead of both gross and net domestic investment with relation
to GNP, [73] much of it seemed to be geared to the export flow. None of the major
turning-points themselves can be explained primarily by the rate of change of consumption plus exports, but the acceleration effect may have contributed to the 1921
up-turn and to the slowness of the upswing in 1923-4. It may have contributed to
the 1929 down-turn also; but, with the sharp rise in the percentage consumed and
the upsurge of retail sales in the middle of the year, on the whole the hypothesis of
insufficient domestic consumption seems inapplicable.

The Keynesian brand of underconsumption theory was more applicable. Innovations
in the automobile, newsprint, hydro-electric power, and non-ferrous metal industries
seem to have been the major cause of the 1921 up-turn. The unfavourable developments in the newsprint and automobile industries, with the consequent effect on the
hydro-electric power industry, were to a great extent responsible for Canada's relatively early down-turn in 1929. [74] A lack of innovation in the 1930's meant that
Canada was more dependent on revival abroad. This strategic role of innovations and
capital glut also fits Schumpeter's and Robertson's theories.

These developments may be translated into the "capital stock" theory. The 1921
depression was a short one partly because Canada's stock of capital had not been increased greatly during the 1919-20 boom and hence favourable investment opportunities
were relatively plentiful. On the other hand, the Canadian capital stock grew
considerably in the 1920's as is evidenced by the relatively large figures for real
net domestic capital formation. Moreover, the proportion of new types of capital
goods in this stock had been increasing considerably during the upswing so that a
longer period might be expected before the up-turn in the 1930's than after the
relatively short post-war boom.

With regard to the 1929 down-turn, it is important to note that the lack of
investment opportunities resulted from the enlarged capital investment in a few
specific industries rather than from a relatively large capital stock in general.

If the capital stock had not been increased so much in the news-print industry, for example, it is improbable that the economically powerful American buyers, with their peculiarly favourable opportunities for manipulating American public opinion, would have been able to force such a sharp price reduction. This fact illustrates the danger of reasoning in terms of aggregates. It is the individual circumstance which counts: the aggregate may well be meaningless without information as to specific industries. The aggregate capital stock may well have been increased in other directions without such depressing effects. [75]

The foreign trade multiplier is basic to an understanding of how cyclical fluctuations are often transmitted from one country to another and how gaps in the balance of payments are narrowed but its implications have by no means been fully analysed. Its working assumes equilibrating capital and/or monetary gold flows so that the transfer and hence multiplication of income may be easily effected. It is often stressed as important because of the determining force which trade flows are presumed to possess over the other items of the international accounts, i.e., because of their supposed ability to induce such equilibrating movements.

This position was held by Keynes [76] (at a time when he did not admit the importance of international shifts of purchasing power as a means of adjustment to gaps in the balance of payments). The opposite view, that the current account is but the result of prior long-term capital movements, is held by Angell, Cassel, Iversen, and Ohlin. [77] Moreover, Tassig, Viner, and White, in their empirical studies, usually consider the long-term capital account as the major disturbing factor and the current account as the induced or equilibrating variable. The rationale of this point of view appears to be that basic changes of the current account balance seldom induce secondary readjustments in the long-term capital account but that basic changes in the long-term capital account always bring about readjusting tendencies in the current account. [78]

The truth would seem to be that either account may predominate and set the pace for the rest of the international accounts. As has been found in the empirical sections, both the long-term capital and the current account may fluctuate in response to cyclical forces primarily rather than to other variables in the international accounts. [79] But one of these two accounts usually could be selected as having played a dominant role within the balance of payments and as having tended to induce equilibrating movements of monetary gold, short-term capital, exchange rates, and thereby to some extent also an equilibrating movement in the other account. In terms of the length of the period of predominance, the current account appears to have been more important [80] since it prevailed throughout the upswing as a whole. But neither school of thought is found wholly correct since it would seem that either account might be the major independent variable (within the international accounts themselves). [81]

Automatic variations of purchasing power [82] seem to have existed throughout. Because of the impossibility of separating the effects of demand changes in the market sense from demand changes involved in shifts of the demand curve, however, it has not been possible to measure the exact comparative strength of this force. Still the shifts-in-demand-schedules mechanism seem to have been a much more potent means of adjustment than price or purchasing power changes dependent upon banking policy since the volume of internal means of payment was altered to con- form with the change in the international flow of reserves in only one instance, 1931-2.

The current account balance is sometimes suggested as the basic variable which exerts the stimulating or depressing force on the home economy. [83] It is the paradox of this Canadian experience, however, that the correlation was usually just the other way round. Generally speaking, the current account balance was most passive when the level of Canadian prosperity was greatest; it was most active when the level of activity was relatively low. Thus, on the whole, the period 1921-5 should have been one of rapid expansion, 1926-9 one of sharp collapse and depression, and 1931-3 one of expansion again if the current account balance be accepted as the criterion of the level of activity. It might be objected that a time-lag would be expected. This is perfectly true -- and if a lag of just some five years (say) be introduced, a generally positive rather than negative correlation between the two series might be obtained. But this surely is too lengthy a lag to allow. Moreover, much the same behaviour is evidenced when the current account computed in real terms is correlated with the level of activity. A much closer correlation existed throughout between total visible and invisible exports on income account and the level of Canadian activity. Thus while a sizeable current account balance may have a stimulating effect on the Canadian economy, the strength of that effect depends upon the absolute level of exports. The importance of the export flow is particularly obvious in the 1933 up-turn when all export categories recovered before or simultaneously with the up-turn of domestic activity. The two previous turning- points were either facilitated directly by strategic export flows or indirectly by some alteration in expectations associated with these strategic exports.

The basic reason for the negative correlation between the current account balance and the level of income is the lag of imports together with the important role of induced domestic investment. When the rise of exports produced a current account surplus in the first half of the upswing, induced domestic investment was low and hence also the demand for imports. When exports rose to a high level, this induced such large domestic investment and hence large import demand that the current account turned passive. When exports fell in the downswing, induced domestic investment fell off much more sharply and hence also import demand so that the current account was rendered progressively less passive.

Table VI is a simplified model of the way in which merchandise exports can stimulate domestic consumption, which might in turn induce domestic investment. It is assumed here (1) that merchandise exports rise by $100 in period one and that this increase is sustained throughout, (2) that the marginal propensity to consume domestic goods is one-half, (3) that induced domestic investment is proportional to the increase in the quantity (exports plus domestic consumption) in the current period, i.e., the "Relation" is one, and (4) that the marginal propensity to import consumers' goods is one-tenth [84] with imports of producers' goods proportional to one-half the increase in domestic investment in each period.

With a $100 increase of merchandise exports induced investment in period one rises by $100 and hence total national income goes up by $200. Resulting from the $100 increase in investment will be a $50 rise in imports and hence a current account balance of $50. With the $100 rise in consumption in period two (one-half of the previous period's increment of income) added to the $100 of exports and resulting $100 induced investment, total national income will be $300 above the original level. The current account balance falls to $30 as consumers' goods imports rise by $20 (one-tenth of the $200 increment of income in the previous period) and producers' goods imports remain at $50. A regular cyclical movement occurs in the national income and in the current account balance, the latter regularly being most active when the national income is lowest and being least active when the national income is highest.

This combination of the Machlup type of analysis with the Samuelson type appears to lead to results more in accord with reality then the simple multiplier sequence. One might be tempted to proceed, varying the assumptions and deducing patterns. But to be realistic, account must be taken of such factors as the following. First, as was seen in the empirical chapters, important elements of domestic investment independent of current consumption and exports may predominate, giving national income a totally different pattern. Secondly, it is more realistic to relate the marginal propensity to consume to some series like disposable income unless the income distribution can be regarded as stable throughout. Similarly, imports of consumers' goods may be a more stable function of disposable income than of national income so that the marginal propensity to import consumers' goods at least should be related to the former. Thirdly, since the induced investment effect of an additional increment of exports or consumption at low levels of activity may well be considerably lower than at higher levels, the magnitude given to the "Relation" must vary. Lastly, when the postulate of stable exchange rates is removed, a series of equations along the lines of those developed by A.J. Brown [85] appears to be a more useful approach.

III. CONCLUSIONS

Some of the more important conclusions are:

(1)   that the cyclical turning-points of a country highly dependent upon external trade may well occasionally precede those in its major markets;

(2)   that no one pattern of expansion need necessarily be associated with economically "young" or "old" countries;

(3)   that no one business cycle theory can be singled out as universally applicable to the complete exclusion of all others; but rather

(4)   that one business cycle theory may explain one turning-point and another theory the next; and

(5)   that different theories may even be applicable to the same turning-point (although one will probably be most pertinent);

(6)   that the monetary theory of business cycle causation does not explain any of the turning-points examined, either through internal bank credit variations or through such movements in "great financial centres";

TABLE VI

Additional National Income Resulting from Autonomous
Export, with Induced Savings, Imports, and Domestic
Investment but No Foreign Repercussions.

(in dollars)

Period	Exports	Current domestic consumption induced (a)	Domestic investment induced (b)	Total imports (c)	Current account balance (1-4)	Total national income (1+2+3)
	(1)	(2)	(3)	(4)	(5)	(6)
1.	100	0.0	100.0	50.0	50.0	200
2.	100	100.0	100.0	70	30.0	300
3.	100	150	50.0	55	45.0	300
4.	100	150	0.0	30	70.0	250
5.	100	125	- 25.0	12.5	87.5	200
6.	100	100	- 25.0	7.5	92.5	175
7.	100	87.5	- 12.5	11.25	88.75	175
8.	100	87.5	0.0	17.5	82.5	187.5
9.	100	93.75	6.25	21.875	78.125	200
10.	100	100.0	6.25	23.125	76.875	206.25
11.	100	103.125	3.125	22.1875	77.8125	206.25
12.	100	103.125	0.0	20.625	79.375	203.125
13.	100	101.5625	- 1.5625	19.53125	80.46875	200.0

(a) The marginal propensity to consume domestic goods is assumed
equal to one-half, consumption being related to income of the previous period.

(b) The "Relation" is assumed to be unity, i.e. domestic investment
currently induced is proportional to the time increase in domestic consumption
plus exports.

(c) The marginal propensity to import consumers' goods is assumed equal
to one-tenth, these imports being related to the income of the previous period.
Imports of producers' goods are assumed to depend upon current investment and
to consist of one-half of current investment.

Conclusions (cont' d)

(7)   that purely psychological theories are also inapplicable;

(8)   that those theories stressing "real" (rather than monetary or psychological) factors are more pertinent, especially the Keynesian-Robertson theory with its stress on innovations, non-cost determinants of investment, and capital glut; but

(9)   that occasionally wage rate changes may have contributed slightly to the turning-points through their effect on business costs;

(10)   that on the whole neither the usual monetary undersaving theory nor Hayek's "Ricardo Effect" is applicable;

(11)   that, although rising long-term capital imports may have facilitated the 1921 up-turn, the collapse of the Canadian boom in 1929 was not caused by any lack of foreign (or domestic) capital;

(12)   that neither income maldistribution nor variations in domestic consumption were prime causes of any of the turning-points;

(13)   that the acceleration principle occasionally helps explain the level of output but the export flow seems a more important determinant of induced investment than variations of domestic consumption;

(14)   that income fluctuations were more important in determining the commodity trade flows than price changes;

(15)   that merchandise exports were a particularly important determinant of the level of activity, especially in the 1933 up-turn but also directly or indirectly in the other turning-points, although rising exports by themselves are not a sufficient condition for widespread prosperity;

(16)   that, with large induced investment, capital imports under paper standard conditions might well have an expansionary influence even in the absence of monetary gold and short-term capital flows;

(17)   that Beach's hypothesis of short-term capital flows as the major independent variable does not apply;

(18)   that short-term capital movements on the whole moved in an equilibrating fashion throughout, not only those so classified in the official estimates but also the "net sales of outstanding securities" and perhaps also the movement of branch plant funds;

(19)   that monetary gold movements also behaved in an equilibrating manner on the whole although they were not as large as the short-term capital flows; but

(20)   that on the whole international movements of monetary reserves did not induce equilibrating variations of internal means of payment or prices and hence that the classical price-specie-flow mechanism of adjustment is inapplicable; and

(21)   that Hawtrey's merchandise and long-term capital models are relevant if brought together in one model and if full allowance is made for automatic purchasing power variations as an adjustment mechanism;

(22)   that especially primary and secondary (multiplier-accelerator) purchasing power effects (as well as altered credit demands resulting from changed marginal efficiencies of capital) are important mechanisms tending to bring about adjustment to balance-of-payments gaps; but

Conclusions (cont' d)

(23)   that the negative correlation of the movements of the current and long-
term capital accounts, in response primarily to the relative speeds of business
expansion at home and abroad, was the most important mechanism tending to
keep the balance of payments in adjustment;

(24)   that any one of the three sector accounts may be the major independent
variable in the international accounts themselves; and

(25)   that Canada's position as a primary producing country was fortunate in
that a sharp diminution of merchandise exports led through the resulting
cyclical downswing and sharply decreased imports to a foreign exchange position
of relative ease.

APPENDIX A

METHOD OF COMPUTATION OF MONTHLY
BALANCE OF PAYMENTS

THIS APPENDIX explains the procedure used in computing the monthly balance of payment figures presented in Tables VII to IX. In every case the monthly estimates have been adjusted so that their total would conform with the yearly estimates. [1]

I. CURRENT ACCOUNT

1. Merchandise trade. The basis used for distributing commodity trade over the months was the trade figures compiled by the Department of Trade and Commerce from the records of the Department of National Revenue. [2] Three statistical difficulties were encountered: (1) the presence of non-commercial items and exclusion of some commercial ones, (2) the distortion involved in fiscal-year-and practices, and (3) the correlation between the time of the customs entry and the exchange market operations connected with any given commodity movement.

First, these trade statistics include such non-commercial items as settlers' effects, free advertising materials, donations of articles from abroad and imports for exhibition purposes which involve no transfer of funds. Moreover, they exclude ship imports. No accurate method of distributing the yearly correction throughout the months presented itself. Hence an arbitrary assumption was made that the correction would fluctuate with the absolute size of the customs trade figure. Thus all the monthly commodity exports and imports have been "corrected" by the percentage that the yearly estimate differed from the yearly customs total.

Secondly, these merchandise export and import figures had also to be adjusted for the abnormality arising from customs arrangements associated with the end of the fiscal year. In an attempt to remove the distortion of March-April trade statistics, [3] 1/7 of March's imports and 1/4 of its exports have been deducted and added to April's figures. A larger fraction of March's exports has been taken because, with navigation on the Great Lakes usually opening up in the last or second last week of March, export volume is exceptionally high in the next month. At the same time imports are fairly constantly received at Canada's borders. Hence a larger fraction of March's exports than of its imports must be taken to make April's trade statistics comparable with those of other months.

Since the exchange market is taken as the point of departure in this study, a third problem arises. Will the exchange market operations connected with exports and imports occur in the same month as the physical movement of these commodities across Canada's border or will there be a lag?

From what information is available, it seems that on the whole the exchange market operations connected with the major part of Canada's exports occur about the same time as the commodities are shipped. Canada's staple exports are financed largely by the discounting of commodity bills. [4] All good Canadian exporting houses have arrangements with their banks permitting them to discount sight or time

bills on good names abroad. [5] These bills pass out of the exchange market at the
time when the banker mails the bills to the other country for collection -- usually
on the day of sale. At this precise moment they are credited to Canada's account
against the rest of the world. Since these bills are discounted at approximately
the same time as the goods are shipped from Canada, the exchange market is
affected at roughly the same time as the physical movement of the exports.

In so far as imports are paid for by bank drafts (usually purchased after the
receipt of the physical goods) or by commodity bills sent to Canada on a collection
basis, the exchange market operations would be carried through at roughly the same
time as the import was received, regardless of its origin. In so far as foreign shippers
discount commodity bills at their banks, the exchange rate would be affected about
the time of the shipment of goods. Since by far the dominant part of Canada's
imports come from the United States, no appreciable lag would be expected between
the time of shipment and the time the goods crossed the Canadian border. Hence,
in the main, the exchange market operations would occur in the same month as the
imports were received.

Thus, because of Canada's geographical position, the structure of its foreign
trade, and the peculiarities of its external trade financing arrangements, it seems
reasonable to use the Customs figures (corrected as above) for any given month for
deriving the merchandise trade statistics in the balance of payments for the same
month.

2.   Commercial gold. Monthly data on the export and import of non-monetary
gold for 1919-25 were also obtained from the Department of Trade and Commerce
reports. Fractional adjustments necessary to make the yearly total equal the yearly
balance of payments figure were made in the November and December figures. The
greatest yearly adjustment necessary was only $0.2 million. Since all figures have
been taken to the nearest tenth of a million and since commercial gold imports
during this period never reached $0.1 million, only commercial gold exports have
been calculated here.

The monthly non-monetary gold export data for 1926-34 had been estimated
by the Bank of Canada research staff. [6] Since the total of these monthly exports
varied but slightly from the latest yearly estimates, [7] only very small adjustments
were necessary.

3.   Freight. Since no monthly or seasonal data on freight receipts or payments
are available, the yearly figures have been distributed over the months according
to certain assumptions.

It is tempting to assume that freight receipts will vary directly with the size of
merchandise exports. Because of the regularity of substantial in-transit railway
traffic across Southwestern Ontario, however, the amplitude of the fluctuation of
freight receipts is much less than that of commodity exports. Receipts from this in-
transit traffic accounted for 36.4, 37.5, 39.3, 40.7, 43.7, 38.0 and 35.8 per
cent respectively of total freight and shipping receipts in the years 1927 to 1934. [8]
Hence this item is assumed to be 40 per cent of total freight receipts for each of the
years. The magnitude of these in-transit receipts would vary with business conditions
in the United States, but evidently the monthly or seasonal fluctuations within any
one year are not large. Hence this 40 per cent of total freight receipts has been

distributed equally over the months. The remaining 60 per cent has been distributed over the months proportionately to the fluctuation in our merchandise exports estimates since most of these freight and shipping earnings are directly connected with the transportation of Canadian exports.

Freight payments are more concentrated in the summer months than merchandise imports because of the relatively large freight paid on American coal (which is usually stocked up at this time) to American shipping and especially railway companies. Freight payments are also slightly heavier in the navigation season because of the high freight rates paid to American companies on other commodities carried across the Great Lakes or down the St. Lawrence River then. The freight paid to American carriers on coal and non-coal imports averaged 65.8 per cent of total freight debits in 1926-35. [9] To increase the incidence of freight payments in the navigation season (and especially in the summer) slightly more than a distribution proportional to commodity imports, one-tenth of gross freight debits has been distributed over the last nine months of each year according to the following schedule; 2, 10, 20, 25, 15, 12, 10, 4, and 2 per cent respectively. The remaining nine-tenths of gross freight debits have been distributed over the months in proportion to the fluctuation in commodity imports.

4. Tourist items. Some monthly tourist data were available. One D.B.S. chart showed the number of entries from the United States for each month of 1944. The monthly number of foreign automobiles in the three classes, local, commercial, and travellers', entering Canada during 1937-43 also was available. [11] The only other monthly distribution available was that of the length of stay of Canadian vehicles in the United States from July 1939 to December 1942. [12] No accurate monthly distribution of tourist expenditures could be made with such data.

Certain facts were obvious, however. American tourists coming by automobile made the greatest expenditures during pre-war years. [13] Moreover, most of them came in the summer months, even in the war year of 1944. [14] In 1937, 78.2 per cent of travellers' vehicle permits issued were for travel during the five months from May to September. [15]

But tourist and other travel expenditures are less concentrated in the summer than is suggested by the number of these travellers' vehicle permits. These permits are designed for the longer-term automobile tourist traffic which is characteristically heavy in the summer months. Business travel, local crossings, and visits between friends and relatives continue throughout the year. In 1946 something between 60 and 70 per cent of United States tourist expenditures in Canada was in the period from May to September [16] This percentage was probably higher in 1926-35 when the Canadian winter tourist industry had not been appreciably developed. It was probably considerably lower in 1920-5 when there were fewer motoring facilities in Canada. Hence it has been conservatively estimated that tourist receipts in the five months from May to September represented 70 per cent of total receipts in 1926-34 and only 50 per cent in 1920-5. The figure corresponding to this percentage has then been distributed among the five months roughly in accordance with the fluctuations in the number of travellers' vehicle permits issued. [17] Since less variation prevails in tourist credits from October to April than in the rest of the

year (except for some concentration in the hunting season, around Christmas, and in
the late spring), the remainder of total tourist credits has been distributed fairly
equally over the remaining months (with only slight increases in the periods mentioned).
The resulting percentage distribution has been 7, 6, 7, 7, 7, 9, 11, 13, 10, 8, 7 and 8 for
each month respectively in 1920-5 and 4, 3, 4, 5, 7, 11, 18, 22, 12, 5, 4, and 5 in
1926-34.

Travel expenditures by Canadians tend to be less concentrated in the summer
because of the year-round attraction of United States metropolitan centres and winter
resorts. In 1946 50 per cent of total tourist debits came in the period May to September.
[18] This summer concentration was probably somewhat less in 1920-5 before summer
automobile touring became popular. The percentage distribution used has been 8,
7, 8, 8, 8, 9, 10, 10, 9, 8, 7 and 8 for each respective month in 1920-5 and 7, 7, 7, 7,
8, 9, 12, 12, 9, 7, 7, and 8 for the following years.

5. Interest and dividends. No monthly or seasonal data on interest and dividend
movements were compiled before the 1939-45 year. Currently, interest payments on
Canadian bonds held abroad tend to cluster in the second and fourth quarters of the
year. It has been assumed that this pattern held in the period under study. Because
interest payments were slightly larger than dividend payments, [19] 54 per cent of
the total interest and dividend debit has been treated as arising from interest payments.
This 54 per cent has been distributed throughout the respective months in the following
schedules: 4, 4, 4, 5, 5, 5, 4, 4, 4, 5, 5, and 5 per cent of the gross debit. Dividend
payments are much heavier in December than in the other months because of year-
end settlements and also tend to concentrate slightly on the first of April, July, and
October. [20] Hence, the remaining 46 per cent of the gross debit has been allocated
according to the following schedule: 3, 3, 3, 4, 3, 3, 4, 3, 3, 4, 3, and 10 per cent
respectively. Only slight differences in percentages have been allowed because
(1) lack of pre-war precludes too great a dependence upon the wartime pattern and
(2) dividends paid to parent companies by subsidiaries, influenced by a variety of
motives and considerations, are not easily predicted. [21] For lack of more information,
it has been assumed that the pattern of interest and dividend receipts was the same as
that of payments.

6. Other current items. The seasonal fluctuation in other current items was not
very large expecially in the earlier years under study, although there was a slight
tendency to concentrate towards the end of the year and to lighten in the summer. [22]
On this basis a very rough distribution has been made. The schedule used was 8, 8, 8,
8, 8, 7, 4, 4, 6, 10, 14 and 15 per cent for each respective month for both other current
credits and debits.

II. BALANCING ITEMS

7. Monetary gold. Monthly estimates of monetary gold imports and exports for
1926-35 have been made by the Bank of Canada research staff. Estimates for 1920-
5 have been made here based upon Viner's method. [23] In brief, following Knox, the
changes in Canada's monetary gold stock have been calculated, the amount of
monetary gold issued by the Mint has been deducted from these monthly changes,
and the resulting figure corrected by the price of the New York dollar in Montreal to
arrive at the value of the monetary gold import or export. In each case the totals

of the monthly figures have almost exactly equalled Knox's yearly estimates except
in 1922 when large gold movements in months of abnormal exchange rates resulted
in a difference of $0.7 million. In all other cases only very slight adjustments were
necessary in the last two months to yield a sum equal to the yearly figure.

8.   Short-term capital. With no adequate monthly data on short-term capital
movements, estimates were made by calculating the changes in the net foreign
balances of the Canadian banking system.[24] These have been adjusted on a pro
rata basis so that the total of all monthly short-term capital movements would yield
the yearly figure.

Short-term capital movements omitted in both the monthly and the yearly balance
of payments figures include (1) those connected with all short-term foreign assets
and liabilities of Canadian individuals, enterprises, and governments which are not
held by Canadian banks and (2) deposits by foreigners of Canadian currency in Canadian banks. Most of such fund transfers by Canadian corporations are included in
the yearly long-term capital account as part of direct investment in subsidiaries
abroad, or as investments of Canadian insurance companies, etc. In the monthly
estimates such short-term movements are included in "all other long-term capital."

III.   LONG-TERM CAPITAL ACCOUNT

9.   New capital imports from the United States, 1920-32. After the 1914-18
war Canadian external borrowings were predominantly from the United States. The
values of monthly placements of Canadian securities in the United States have been
compiled from the Commercial and Financial Chronicle.[25] Only new capital issues
have been selected; refunding issues were ignored because of the greater likelihood
of error in assuming that the funds came to Canada immediately. It has been arbitrarily assumed that only 95 per cent of these new capital placements formed an
immediate movement of long-term capital to Canada, the rest going for commissions
of such expenses. It has also been arbitrarily assumed that half of a month's placements formed a long-term capital movement in the same month and half in the
following month. The resulting figures have been corrected by the price of New
York funds in Montreal to arrive at the imports of "new" United States capital. This
account has not been given for the years 1933-4 since only one new capital flotation
of minor size ($0.1 million) occurred then.

10.   All other long-term capital, 1920-32. Of the remaining items of the
long-term capital account, the two most important are "maturities and redemptions
of Canadian securities abroad" and "net sales of outstanding securities." With no
adequate data available for 1920-32, resort has been made to the "indirect method"
of estimating all other capital movements. The balancing items, the current
account balance, and new United States capital imports have been summed and the
sign changed to yield the movements of "all other long-term capital."

The residual item has not been shown separately in the monthly estimates but
has been included in the series "all other long-term capital" because it seems to
be attributable, to some degree at least, to unrecorded movements of outstanding
securities. [26] Since the whole of the residual item cannot be explained satisfactorily

by this means, [27] the resulting monthly capital figures must be considered as unduly conservative in such years as 1921-2 which had large debit residuals.

11. Sales and purchases of outstanding securities, 1933-4. D.B.S. has compiled monthly data on the sales and purchases of outstanding securities starting from January 1933. [28] These estimates are included in the capital account tables here for these two years.

12. Remaining capital items, 1933-4. This category has been obtained by the method used in computing "all other long-term capital" for 1920-32 with two exceptions: (1) the net sales and purchases of outstanding securities have also been deducted and (2) new long-term capital imports from the United States ($0.1 million) have been included. As before, the residual is included.

TABLE VII
Canadian Monthly Current Account, 1920-34
(in millions of dollars)

C = credits (+) D = debits (-) ID = interest and dividends CG = commercial gold (net credits) B = Balance

Month	Trade C	Trade D	Travel C	Travel D	ID C	ID D	Freight C	Freight D	CG	Other C	Other D	Total C	Total D	B
1920														
Jan.	116.4	110.7	6.4	5.0	3.3	14.9	10.1	11.9	1.4	3.6	4.0	111.2	146.5	5.3 −
Feb.	85.8	93.5	5.5	4.4	3.3	14.9	8.4	10.0	.8	3.6	4.0	107.4	126.8	19.4 −
March	69.4	130.5	6.4	5.0	3.3	14.9	7.6	14.0	.4	3.6	4.0	90.7	168.4	77.7 −
April	76.3	126.8	6.4	5.0	4.2	19.2	7.9	13.9	.3	3.6	4.0	98.7	168.9	70.2 −
May	76.9	121.1	6.4	5.0	3.7	17.0	8.0	14.7	.3	3.6	4.0	98.9	161.8	62.9 −
June	106.1	143.9	8.2	5.6	3.7	17.0	9.5	18.8	.3	3.2	3.5	131.0	188.8	57.8 −
July	104.7	136.0	11.0	6.3	3.7	17.0	9.5	18.9	.1	1.8	2.0	130.8	180.2	49.4 −
August	111.9	132.8	11.0	6.3	3.3	14.9	9.9	16.8	.3	1.8	2.0	138.2	172.8	34.6 −
Sept.	94.2	123.0	9.1	5.6	3.3	14.9	8.9	15.2	.1	2.7	3.0	118.3	161.7	43.4 −
Oct.	129.1	113.1	7.3	5.0	4.2	19.2	10.8	13.8	.1	4.6	4.9	156.1	156.0	.1 +
Nov.	147.2	105.5	6.4	4.4	3.7	17.0	11.9	12.0	.2	6.5	6.8	175.9	145.7	30.2 +
Dec.	149.1	91.3	7.3	4.9	7.1	32.0	11.9	10.1	.3	6.9	7.2	182.6	146.0	36.6 +
Total...	1,267.1	1,428.7	91.4	62.5	46.8	212.9	114.4	170.1	4.6	45.5	49.4	1,569.8	1,923.6	353.8 −
1921														
Jan.	80.6	74.9	6.9	4.6	3.3	16.4	7.9	9.5	.3	3.2	2.7	102.2	108.1	5.9 −
Feb.	64.9	74.5	5.9	4.0	3.3	16.4	6.9	9.4	.3	3.2	2.7	84.5	107.0	22.5 −
March	50.8	82.2	6.9	4.6	3.3	16.4	6.0	10.4	.4	3.2	2.7	70.6	116.3	45.7 −
April	60.0	81.3	6.9	4.6	4.3	21.1	6.6	10.5	.2	3.2	2.7	81.2	120.2	39.0 −
May	59.1	70.9	6.9	4.6	3.9	18.7	6.6	10.2	.2	2.8	2.7	80.2	107.1	26.9 −
June	58.3	59.6	8.8	5.2	3.9	18.7	6.5	9.8	.3	2.8	2.4	80.6	95.7	15.1 −
July	54.3	64.6	11.8	5.8	3.9	18.7	6.2	11.1	.2	1.6	1.3	78.0	101.5	23.5 −
August	61.4	67.4	11.8	5.8	3.3	16.4	6.7	10.3	.1	1.6	1.3	84.9	101.2	16.3 −
Sept.	58.2	61.9	9.8	5.2	3.3	16.4	6.5	9.2	.1	2.4	2.0	80.3	94.7	14.4 −
Oct.	79.7	61.6	7.9	4.6	4.3	21.1	7.8	9.0	.2	4.0	3.4	103.9	99.7	4.2 +
Nov.	86.5	66.6	6.8	4.0	3.7	18.8	8.3	8.9	.1	5.8	4.7	111.2	103.0	8.2 +
Dec.	86.3	62.3	7.8	4.5	6.8	35.2	8.3	8.2	.1	6.2	5.1	115.5	115.3	.2 +
Total...	800.4	827.8	98.2	57.5	47.3	234.3	84.3	116.5	2.5	40.4	33.7	1,073.1	1,269.8	196.7 −
1922														
Jan.	46.2	50.3	7.7	4.5	2.8	16.1	5.1	5.7	.2	3.1	2.1	65.1	78.7	13.6 −
Feb.	45.8	53.0	6.6	4.0	2.8	16.1	5.0	6.0	.4	3.1	2.1	63.7	81.2	17.5 −
March	44.6	66.4	7.7	4.5	2.8	16.1	5.0	7.6	.3	3.1	2.1	63.5	96.7	33.2 −
April	46.6	57.7	7.7	4.5	3.6	20.7	5.1	6.8	.3	3.1	2.1	66.4	91.8	25.4 −
May	69.1	64.5	7.7	5.1	3.2	18.4	6.3	8.3	.3	2.7	1.9	89.7	97.8	8.1 −
June	71.7	60.2	9.9	5.7	3.2	18.4	6.4	8.8	.4	1.5	1.1	94.3	94.4	.1 +
July	70.4	59.1	13.3	5.7	3.2	18.4	6.4	9.2	.3	1.5	1.1	95.1	93.8	1.3 +
August	73.4	65.8	13.3	5.7	2.3	16.1	6.5	8.9	.3	1.5	1.1	97.8	97.6	.2 +
Sept.	71.6	58.9	11.1	5.1	2.8	16.1	6.4	7.8	.4	2.3	1.6	94.5	89.5	5.0 +
Oct.	102.7	65.3	8.8	4.5	3.6	20.7	8.1	8.3	.4	3.4	2.7	127.4	101.5	25.9 +
Nov.	131.1	74.5	7.8	4.1	3.2	18.5	9.7	8.9	.3	5.4	3.8	157.5	109.3	47.7 +
Dec.	110.9	68.6	8.9	4.6	5.9	34.7	8.5	8.0	.5	5.7	4.1	140.4	120.0	20.4 +

TABLE VII (Cont'd.)

Month	Trade C	Trade D	Travel C	Travel D	ID C	ID D	Freight C	Freight D	CG C	Other C	Other D	Total C	Total D	B
1923														
Jan.	64.4	66.7	9.1	4.9	2.8	17.8	6.4	8.2	.4	3.7	1.5	86.8	99.1	12.3 −
Feb.	57.0	64.0	7.8	4.3	2.8	17.8	6.0	7.9	.8	3.7	1.5	78.1	95.5	17.4 −
March	56.5	77.1	9.1	4.9	2.8	17.8	6.0	9.5	1.3	3.7	1.5	79.4	110.8	31.4 −
April	71.9	79.7	9.1	4.9	3.6	22.9	6.8	10.0	.7	3.7	1.5	95.8	119.0	23.2 −
May	73.1	82.6	9.1	4.9	3.2	20.3	6.9	11.4	1.8	3.7	1.5	97.8	120.7	22.9 −
June	93.1	82.9	11.8	5.6	3.2	20.3	8.0	12.6	1.9	3.2	1.3	121.2	122.7	1.5 −
July	81.2	75.5	15.7	6.2	3.2	20.3	7.3	12.3	1.9	1.8	.7	111.1	115.0	3.9 −
August	79.8	77.2	15.7	6.2	2.8	17.8	7.3	11.3	.3	1.8	.7	107.7	113.2	5.5 −
Sept.	67.4	69.9	13.1	5.6	2.8	17.8	6.6	10.1	.3	2.8	1.1	93.0	104.5	11.5 −
Oct.	100.1	74.7	10.5	4.9	3.6	22.9	8.3	10.4	.1	4.6	1.3	127.2	114.7	12.5 +
Nov.	137.2	70.6	9.1	4.4	3.4	20.3	10.1	9.3	1.1	5.5	2.6	167.4	107.2	60.2 +
Dec.	122.2	64.2	10.6	5.0	6.3	38.0	9.5	8.4	1.9	6.9	2.6	157.4	118.2	39.2 +
Total...	1,003.9	885.1	130.7	61.8	40.5	254.0	89.2	121.4	12.5	46.1	18.3	1,322.9	1,340.6	17.7 −
1924														
Jan.	67.3	65.1	10.5	5.5	2.8	17.0	6.0	7.4	2.5	3.9	1.9	93.0	96.9	3.9 −
Feb.	65.4	60.7	9.0	4.8	2.8	17.0	6.0	6.9	2.1	3.9	1.9	89.2	91.3	2.1 −
March	67.4	72.9	10.5	5.5	2.8	17.0	6.1	8.2	2.7	3.9	1.9	93.4	105.5	12.1 −
April	69.8	70.9	10.5	5.5	3.6	21.8	6.2	8.2	1.7	3.9	1.9	95.7	108.3	12.6 −
May	102.2	70.5	10.5	5.5	3.2	19.4	7.7	9.0	2.3	3.9	1.9	129.8	106.3	23.5 +
June	85.4	64.9	13.4	6.1	3.2	19.4	6.9	9.3	2.6	3.4	1.6	114.3	101.3	13.0 +
July	84.7	71.0	17.9	6.8	3.2	19.4	6.9	10.5	2.0	1.9	.9	117.2	108.6	8.6 +
August	71.9	60.6	17.9	6.8	2.8	17.0	6.3	8.3	2.1	1.9	.9	102.9	93.6	9.3 +
Sept.	79.0	62.5	14.9	6.1	2.8	17.0	6.6	8.3	2.2	1.9	.9	108.4	95.3	13.1 +
Oct.	101.0	65.7	12.0	5.5	3.6	21.8	7.7	8.5	2.6	2.9	1.4	131.7	104.9	26.8 +
Nov.	116.7	64.7	10.4	4.8	3.3	19.3	8.2	7.7	2.6	4.8	2.4	148.0	99.8	48.2 +
Dec.	121.8	59.4	11.9	5.4	6.2	36.2	8.4	6.8	2.9	6.8	3.3	158.3	111.3	47.0 +
Total...	1,032.6	789.9	149.4	68.3	40.3	242.3	83.0	99.1	28.3	48.3	23.5	1,381.9	1,223.1	158.8 +
1925														
Jan.	73.0	57.2	11.9	5.6	2.8	17.5	6.0	6.3	2.4	4.3	3.2	100.4	89.8	10.6 +
Feb.	68.0	60.2	10.2	4.9	2.8	17.5	5.7	6.6	2.2	4.3	3.2	93.2	92.4	.8 +
March	68.8	71.1	11.9	5.6	2.8	17.5	5.8	7.8	3.1	4.3	3.2	96.7	105.2	8.5 −
April	80.8	69.7	11.9	5.6	3.6	22.6	6.3	7.9	2.5	4.3	3.2	109.1	109.0	.1 +
May	94.0	74.4	11.9	5.6	3.2	20.1	6.8	9.3	2.5	4.3	2.8	122.7	112.6	10.1 +
June	90.7	74.1	15.3	6.3	3.2	20.1	6.7	10.2	2.9	3.7	2.8	122.5	113.5	9.0 +
July	99.2	79.9	20.4	7.0	3.2	20.1	7.1	11.5	2.6	2.1	1.6	134.6	120.1	14.5 +
August	108.0	80.4	20.4	7.0	2.8	17.5	7.4	10.4	3.5	2.1	1.6	144.2	116.9	27.3 +
Sept.	105.6	77.1	17.0	6.3	3.6	22.6	7.3	9.8	3.0	3.2	2.4	138.9	113.1	25.8 +
Oct.	141.2	79.2	13.6	5.6	3.6	22.6	8.8	9.8	2.5	5.4	3.9	175.1	121.1	54.0 +
Nov.	137.5	73.8	12.1	4.8	3.3	20.1	8.7	8.5	3.0	7.5	5.4	172.1	112.6	59.5 +
Dec.	174.3	75.3	13.8	5.4	6.1	37.6	10.1	8.3	1.6	8.0	5.7	213.9	132.3	81.6 +
Total...	1,241.1	872.4	170.4	69.7	40.2	250.7	86.7	106.4	31.5	53.5	39.4	1,623.4	1,338.6	284.8 +

TABLE VII (Cont'd.)

Month	Trade C	Trade D	Travel C	Travel D	ID C	ID D	Freight C	Freight D	CG C	CG D	Other C	Other D	Total C	Total D		B
1926																
Jan.	84.9	67.3	6.1	6.9	2.2	16.8	7.0	6.5	1.1	6.6	6.6	9.7	107.9	107.2	+	.7
Feb.	88.1	68.4	4.6	6.9	2.2	16.8	7.2	6.6	2.5	6.6	6.6	9.7	111.2	108.4	+	2.8
March	84.7	83.5	6.1	6.9	2.2	16.8	7.0	8.1	1.0	6.6	6.6	9.7	107.6	125.0	-	17.4
April	88.5	79.3	7.6	6.9	2.9	21.6	7.2	7.9	3.0	6.6	6.6	9.7	115.8	125.4	-	9.6
May	92.2	83.1	10.6	7.9	2.6	19.2	7.4	9.2	2.8	6.6	6.6	9.7	122.2	129.1	-	6.9
June	118.3	88.3	16.7	8.9	2.6	19.2	8.6	10.7	2.6	5.8	5.8	8.5	154.6	135.6	+	19.0
July	110.6	85.5	27.4	11.9	2.6	19.2	8.2	10.9	3.1	3.3	3.3	4.8	155.2	132.3	+	22.9
August	90.9	86.6	33.4	11.9	2.2	16.8	7.3	10.0	2.6	3.3	3.3	4.8	139.7	130.1	+	9.6
Sept.	92.4	82.6	18.2	8.9	2.2	16.8	7.4	9.3	3.2	5.0	5.0	7.3	128.4	124.9	+	3.5
Oct.	130.3	85.0	7.6	6.9	2.9	21.6	9.1	9.4	2.8	8.3	8.3	12.1	161.0	135.0	+	26.0
Nov.	152.6	84.6	6.1	7.0	2.6	19.2	10.1	8.6	2.7	11.7	11.7	16.9	185.8	136.3	+	49.5
Dec.	138.5	78.8	7.6	8.0	4.8	36.0	9.5	7.8	2.6	12.6	12.6	18.1	175.6	148.7	+	26.9
Total...	1,272.0	973.0	152.0	99.0	32.0	240.0	96.0	105.0	30.0	83.0	83.0	121.0	1,665.0	1,538.0	+	127.0
1927																
Jan.	83.7	76.6	6.5	7.0	2.9	18.0	7.2	7.1	3.0	6.8	6.8	9.6	110.1	118.3	-	8.2
Feb.	78.3	72.6	4.9	7.0	2.9	18.0	7.0	6.7	2.8	6.8	6.8	9.6	102.7	113.9	-	11.2
March	78.8	92.1	6.5	7.0	2.9	18.0	7.0	8.5	3.3	6.8	6.8	9.6	105.3	135.2	-	29.9
April	103.2	87.6	8.2	7.0	3.7	23.1	8.1	8.3	2.9	6.8	6.8	9.6	132.9	135.6	-	2.7
May	109.2	91.8	11.4	8.0	3.3	20.6	8.4	9.6	3.1	6.8	6.8	9.6	142.2	139.6	+	2.6
June	105.2	98.2	17.9	9.0	3.3	20.6	8.2	11.3	2.5	6.0	6.0	8.4	143.1	147.5	-	4.4
July	79.2	88.1	29.3	12.0	3.3	20.6	7.0	10.6	2.9	3.4	3.4	4.8	125.1	136.4	-	11.3
August	94.1	96.6	35.9	12.0	2.9	18.0	7.7	10.6	2.7	3.4	3.4	4.8	146.7	142.0	+	4.7
Sept.	97.4	89.3	19.6	9.0	2.9	18.0	7.9	9.6	3.4	5.1	5.1	7.2	136.3	133.1	+	3.2
Oct.	103.8	91.3	8.2	7.0	3.7	23.1	8.2	9.6	3.0	8.5	8.5	12.0	135.4	143.0	-	7.6
Nov.	152.5	91.7	6.5	7.0	3.2	20.5	10.7	8.9	-.5	11.9	11.9	16.8	184.3	144.9	+	39.4
Dec.	129.6	81.1	8.1	8.0	6.0	38.5	9.6	7.9	2.9	12.7	12.7	18.0	168.9	153.5	+	15.4
Total...	1,215.0	1,057.0	163.0	100.0	41.0	257.0	97.0	109.0	32.0	85.0	85.0	120.0	1,633.0	1,643.0	-	10.0
1928																
Jan.	82.4	78.6	7.1	6.9	3.2	19.3	6.7	6.8	7.8	7.0	7.0	9.6	114.2	121.4	-	7.2
Feb.	88.2	85.1	5.3	6.9	3.2	19.3	7.0	7.3	3.0	7.0	7.0	9.8	113.7	128.4	-	14.7
March	79.9	102.2	7.1	6.9	3.2	19.3	6.6	8.8	3.0	7.0	7.0	9.8	106.8	147.0	-	40.2
April	85.7	94.6	8.9	6.9	4.1	24.8	6.9	8.4	2.6	7.0	7.0	9.8	115.2	144.5	-	29.3
May	117.3	112.4	12.4	7.8	3.7	22.0	8.2	10.9	3.1	7.0	7.0	9.8	151.7	162.9	-	11.2
June	106.5	109.5	19.3	8.8	3.7	22.0	7.8	11.8	2.8	6.2	6.2	8.5	146.3	160.6	-	14.3
July	124.3	102.3	31.9	11.8	3.7	22.0	8.5	11.9	3.0	3.5	3.5	4.9	174.9	152.9	+	22.0
August	111.1	113.0	38.9	11.8	3.2	22.0	8.0	11.5	2.8	3.5	3.5	4.9	167.5	160.5	+	7.0
Sept.	109.2	104.9	21.2	8.8	3.2	19.3	7.9	10.8	3.2	5.3	5.3	7.3	150.0	150.8	-	.8
Oct.	140.4	111.1	8.9	6.9	4.1	24.8	9.2	10.8	2.8	8.8	8.8	12.2	174.2	165.8	+	8.4
Nov.	166.0	101.8	7.1	6.8	3.7	21.8	10.3	9.2	3.2	12.4	12.4	17.0	202.7	156.6	+	46.1
Dec.	130.0	93.5	8.9	7.7	7.0	41.1	8.9	8.1	2.7	13.3	13.3	18.2	170.8	166.6	+	2.2
Total...	1,341.0	1,209.0	177.0	98.0	46.0	275.0	96.0	116.0	40.0	88.0	88.0	122.0	1,788.0	1,820.0	-	32.0

TABLE VII (cont'd.)

Month	Trade C	Trade D	Travel C	Travel D	ID C	ID D	Freight C	Freight D	CG	Other C	Other D	Total C	Total D	B
1929														
Jan.	94.9	95.0	7.9	7.6	4.3	22.5	7.6	8.7	1.4	6.4	10.0	122.5	143.8	21.3
Feb.	81.7	95.0	5.9	7.6	4.3	22.5	6.9	8.7	5.3	6.4	10.0	110.5	143.8	33.3
March	85.9	113.6	7.9	7.6	4.3	22.5	7.1	10.4	3.5	6.4	10.0	115.1	164.1	49.0
April	94.2	114.4	9.9	7.6	5.5	29.0	7.5	10.8	2.5	6.4	10.0	126.0	171.8	45.8
May	106.7	123.0	13.9	8.6	4.9	25.8	8.1	12.6	3.3	6.4	10.0	143.3	180.0	36.7
June	111.6	109.6	21.8	9.7	4.9	25.8	8.3	12.7	3.1	5.6	8.8	155.3	166.6	11.3
July	103.0	111.8	35.6	13.0	4.9	25.8	7.9	13.6	2.9	3.2	5.0	157.5	169.2	11.7
August	95.9	109.3	43.6	13.0	4.3	22.5	7.6	12.1	2.9	3.2	5.0	157.5	161.9	4.4
Sept.	87.2	97.3	23.8	9.7	4.3	22.5	7.2	10.5	3.3	4.8	7.5	130.6	147.5	16.9
Oct.	118.4	113.9	9.9	7.6	5.5	29.0	8.7	11.8	3.3	8.0	12.5	153.7	174.8	21.1
Nov.	110.4	106.4	7.9	7.5	4.4	25.8	8.1	10.3	3.1	11.2	17.5	145.5	167.5	22.0
Dec.	88.1	82.7	9.9	8.5	9.0	48.3	7.0	7.8	2.5	12.0	18.7	128.5	166.0	37.5
Total...	1,178.0	1,272.0	198.0	108.0	61.0	322.0	92.0	130.0	37.0	80.0	125.0	1,646.0	1,957.0	311.0
1930														
Jan.	73.3	81.7	7.2	6.4	4.1	24.4	5.8	7.8	3.6	5.5	9.4	99.5	129.7	30.2
Feb.	66.2	78.1	5.4	6.4	4.1	24.4	5.5	7.4	2.6	5.5	7.4	89.3	125.7	36.4
March	66.8	93.4	7.2	6.4	4.1	24.4	5.5	8.9	3.4	5.5	9.4	92.5	142.5	50.0
April	73.3	84.5	9.0	7.4	5.3	31.3	5.8	8.3	3.0	5.5	9.4	101.9	139.9	38.0
May	77.3	97.9	12.6	7.4	4.7	27.8	6.0	10.3	3.1	4.8	9.4	109.1	152.8	43.7
June	78.2	88.3	19.8	8.3	4.7	27.8	6.0	10.5	3.2	2.8	8.3	116.6	143.2	26.6
July	75.7	81.6	32.4	11.0	4.7	27.8	5.9	10.4	3.2	2.8	4.7	124.7	135.5	10.8
August	68.6	75.2	39.6	11.0	4.1	24.4	5.6	8.7	3.2	4.1	4.7	123.7	124.0	.3
Sept.	79.9	84.8	21.6	8.3	4.1	24.4	6.1	9.3	3.2	4.1	7.1	119.0	133.9	14.9
Oct.	81.9	75.6	9.0	6.4	5.3	31.3	6.2	8.2	3.7	6.9	11.8	113.0	133.3	20.3
Nov.	72.6	73.6	7.2	6.5	4.8	27.8	6.0	7.4	3.3	9.7	16.6	103.6	131.9	28.3
Dec.	66.2	58.3	9.0	7.5	9.0	52.2	5.6	5.8	3.9	10.4	17.8	104.1	141.6	37.5
Total...	880.0	973.0	180.0	92.0	59.0	348.0	70.0	103.0	39.0	69.0	118.0	1,297.0	1,634.0	337.0
1931														
Jan.	44.4	46.5	6.1	5.0	3.4	23.1	4.2	5.7	4.3	4.7	6.9	67.1	87.2	20.1
Feb.	43.7	47.1	4.6	5.0	3.4	23.1	4.2	5.8	3.6	4.7	6.9	64.2	87.9	23.7
March	41.1	59.7	6.1	5.0	3.4	23.1	4.0	7.3	3.8	4.7	6.9	63.1	102.0	38.9
April	47.5	57.2	7.7	5.7	4.3	29.7	4.4	7.2	3.9	4.7	6.9	72.5	106.0	33.5
May	59.2	67.9	10.7	5.7	3.8	26.4	5.0	9.1	3.8	4.1	6.0	87.2	116.0	28.8
June	53.8	48.5	16.8	6.4	3.8	26.4	4.7	7.5	3.9	4.1	6.0	87.1	94.8	7.7
July	49.3	44.7	27.5	8.5	3.8	26.4	4.5	7.5	4.5	2.4	3.4	92.0	90.5	1.5
August	48.6	43.7	33.7	8.5	3.4	23.1	4.5	6.6	4.5	2.4	3.4	97.0	85.3	11.7
Sept.	48.6	41.9	18.4	6.4	3.4	23.1	4.4	6.0	7.3	3.5	5.2	85.6	82.6	3.0
Oct.	55.0	42.4	7.7	5.0	4.3	29.7	4.8	6.0	10.8	5.9	8.6	88.5	91.7	3.2
Nov.	56.9	43.3	6.1	5.0	3.8	26.4	4.9	5.6	4.4	8.3	12.0	84.4	92.3	7.9
Dec.	52.9	37.1	7.6	5.5	7.2	49.5	4.5	4.7	2.2	8.9	12.9	83.3	109.7	26.4
Total...	601.0	580.0	153.0	71.0	48.0	330.0	54.0	79.0	57.0	59.0	86.0	972.0	1,146.0	174.0

TABLE VII (Cont'd.)

Month	Trade C	Trade D	Travel C	Travel D	ID C	ID D	Freight C	Freight D	CG	Other C	Other D	Total C	Total D		B
1932															
Jan.	38.6	30.0	4.6	3.4	2.6	21.1	3.1	4.5	4.0	4.3	7.1	57.2	66.1	−	8.9
Feb.	36.5	31.3	3.4	3.4	2.6	21.1	3.0	4.7	6.3	4.3	7.1	56.1	67.6	−	11.5
March	30.3	43.3	4.6	3.4	2.6	21.1	2.7	6.5	5.9	4.3	7.1	50.4	81.4	−	31.0
April	37.1	33.4	5.7	3.4	3.3	27.2	3.0	5.1	4.6	4.3	7.1	58.0	76.2	−	18.2
May	40.7	39.0	8.0	3.9	3.0	24.2	3.2	6.5	5.9	4.3	7.1	65.1	80.7	−	15.6
June	41.0	35.8	12.5	4.4	3.0	24.2	3.2	6.6	6.5	3.8	6.2	70.0	77.2	−	7.2
July	42.4	31.4	20.5	5.9	3.0	24.2	3.3	6.4	3.8	2.8	3.6	75.2	71.5	+	3.7
August	41.3	32.1	25.1	5.9	2.6	21.1	3.2	5.8	6.2	2.2	3.6	80.6	68.5	+	12.1
Sept.	42.1	30.3	13.7	4.4	2.6	21.1	3.2	5.3	7.7	3.2	5.3	72.5	66.4	+	6.1
Oct.	56.4	32.6	5.7	3.4	3.3	27.2	3.9	5.6	3.2	5.4	8.9	77.9	77.7	+	.2
Nov.	46.0	33.2	4.6	3.4	3.0	24.2	3.2	5.3	7.7	7.6	12.5	72.1	78.6	−	6.5
Dec.	42.6	25.6	5.6	4.1	5.4	45.3	3.0	3.7	8.2	8.1	13.4	72.9	92.1	−	19.2
Total...	495.0	398.0	114.0	49.0	37.0	302.0	38.0	66.0	70.0	54.0	89.0	808.0	904.0	−	96.0
1933															
Jan.	31.7	22.4	3.6	3.1	2.7	18.5	3.1	3.6	6.2	3.5	7.1	50.8	54.7	−	3.9
Feb.	26.5	21.6	2.7	3.1	2.7	18.5	2.8	3.5	5.1	3.5	7.1	43.3	53.8	−	10.5
March	27.6	26.0	3.6	3.1	2.7	18.5	2.9	4.2	5.6	3.5	7.1	45.9	58.9	−	13.0
April	29.3	23.1	4.5	3.1	3.4	23.8	3.0	3.8	5.9	3.5	7.1	49.6	60.9	−	11.3
May	45.6	30.2	6.2	3.5	3.0	21.1	3.8	5.6	9.4	3.5	7.1	71.5	67.5	+	4.0
June	46.0	30.8	9.8	4.0	3.0	21.1	3.8	6.3	5.8	3.1	6.2	71.5	68.4	+	3.1
July	51.3	32.7	16.0	5.3	3.0	21.1	4.0	7.0	7.1	1.8	3.6	83.2	69.7	+	13.5
August	44.6	35.5	19.6	5.3	2.7	18.5	3.7	6.7	6.7	1.8	3.6	79.1	69.6	+	9.5
Sept.	57.7	35.5	10.7	4.0	2.7	18.5	4.4	6.5	9.1	2.6	5.3	87.2	69.8	+	17.4
Oct.	60.3	37.7	4.5	3.1	3.4	23.8	4.5	6.8	7.7	4.4	8.9	84.8	80.3	+	4.5
Nov.	60.2	40.1	3.5	3.1	3.0	21.1	4.3	6.8	9.9	6.2	12.5	87.1	83.6	+	3.5
Dec.	51.2	32.4	4.3	3.3	5.7	39.5	3.7	5.2	3.5	6.6	13.4	75.0	93.8	−	18.8
Total...	532.0	368.0	89.0	44.0	38.0	264.0	44.0	66.0	82.0	44.0	89.0	829.0	831.0	−	2.0
1934															
Jan.	46.3	30.5	4.2	3.5	4.0	18.8	3.9	4.5	9.3	3.4	5.7	71.1	63.0	+	8.1
Feb.	37.7	31.7	3.2	3.5	4.0	18.8	3.5	4.7	17.5	3.4	5.7	69.3	64.4	+	4.9
March	43.0	38.4	4.2	3.5	4.0	18.8	3.8	5.6	12.3	3.4	5.7	70.7	72.0	−	1.3
April	45.7	39.2	5.3	3.5	5.1	24.1	3.9	6.0	7.0	3.4	5.7	70.4	78.5	−	8.1
May	57.4	49.9	7.4	4.0	4.6	21.4	4.5	8.1	9.4	3.4	5.7	86.7	89.1	−	2.4
June	57.5	43.5	11.7	4.5	4.6	21.4	4.5	8.0	8.8	3.0	5.0	90.1	82.4	+	7.7
July	55.8	41.6	19.1	6.0	4.6	21.4	4.4	8.1	8.7	1.7	2.8	94.3	79.9	+	14.4
August	54.8	41.0	23.3	6.0	4.0	18.8	4.3	7.2	10.4	1.7	2.8	98.5	75.8	+	22.7
Sept.	57.7	39.8	12.7	4.5	4.0	18.8	4.5	6.7	5.9	2.6	4.3	87.4	74.1	+	13.3
Oct.	67.1	44.5	5.3	3.5	5.1	24.1	4.9	7.3	9.9	4.3	7.1	96.6	86.5	+	10.1
Nov.	64.5	47.0	4.2	3.5	4.6	21.4	5.0	7.2	7.9	6.0	9.9	92.2	89.0	+	3.2
Dec.	60.5	36.9	5.4	4.0	8.4	40.2	4.8	5.6	6.9	6.7	10.6	92.7	97.3	−	4.6
Total ..	648.0	484.0	106.0	50.0	57.0	268.0	52.0	79.0	114.0	43.0	71.0	1,020.0	952.0	+	68.0

TABLE VIII

Canadian Monthly Short - and Long-Term Capital Accounts, 1920-32
(in millions of dollars)

MG=Monetary gold   SC=Short-term capital   fUS= New imports from the United
States   AO= All other   T=Total   + = Credit   - = Debit

Month	Balancing items			Long-term capital		
	MG	SC	T	fUS	AO	T
1920						
J	+ 11.2	+ 10.7	+ 21.9			- 16.6
F	+ .3	+ 7.8	+ 8.1			+ 11.3
M	+ 6.5	+ 13.3	+ 19.8			+ 57.9
A	- 4.1	+ 17.8	+ 13.7			+ 56.5
M	- 7.6	+ 19.8	+ 12.2			+ 50.7
J	+ 20.3	- 9.2	+ 11.1			+ 46.7
J	+ 2.1	+ 6.2	+ 8.3			+ 41.1
A	+ 1.5	+ 9.0	+ 10.5			+ 24.1
S	+ .6	+ 28.4	+ 29.0			+ 14.4
O	+ 1.0	- 22.7	- 21.7			+ 21.6
N	- .3	- 9.9	- 10.2			- 20.0
D	- 1.1	- 28.8	- 29.9			- 6.7
Total	+ 30.4	+ 42.4	+ 72.8			+281.0
1921						
J	- .1	+ 16.6	+ 16.5	+ 15.0	- 25.6	- 10.6
F	+ .3	+ 19.3	+ 19.6	+ 11.0	- 8.1	+ 2.9
M	+ 19.1	+ 4.9	+ 24.0	+ 6.0	+ 15.7	+ 21.7
A	+ 4.7	+ 20.0	+ 24.7	+ 7.0	+' 7.3	+ 14.3
M	+ .1	+ 10.2	+ 10.3	+ 3.1	+ 13.5	+ 16.6
J	+ 4.7	+ 18.1	+ 22.8	+ 4.4	- 12.1	- 7.7
J	+ .3	+ 8.2	+ 8.5	+ 18.8	- 3.8	+ 15.0
A	+ 5.0	+ 20.2	+ 25.2	+ 17.8	- 26.7	- 8.9
S	+ 3.5	+ 9.3	+ 12.8	+ 33.3	- 31.7	+ 1.6
O	+ 1.3	+ 3.6	+ 4.9	+ 33.6	- 42.7	- 9.1
N	+ .4	+ 11.2	+ 11.6	+ 10.2	- 30.0	- 19.8
D	+ .2	+ 2.8	+ 3.0	+ 21.6	- 24.8	- 3.2
Total	+ 39.5	+144.4	+183.9	+181.8	-169.0	+ 12.8

TABLE VIII (cont'd)

Month	Balancing items			Long-term capital		
	MG	SC	T	fUS	AO	T
1922						
J	+ 2.6	+ 13.2	+ 15.8	+ 24.7	- 26.9	- 2.2
F	+ 1.6	+ 2.0	+ 3.6	+ 10.3	+ 3.6	+ 13.9
M	+ 1.5	+ 20.7	+ 22.2	+ 12.7	- 1.7	+ 11.0
A	+ 1.2	+ 4.7	+ 5.9	+ 24.3	- 4.8	+ 19.5
M	- .7	+ 10.7	+ 10.0	+ 18.3	- 20.2	- 1.9
J	- .1	+ 2.1	+ 2.0	+ 8.9	- 10.8	- 1.9
J	- .2	- 7.0	- 7.2	+ 6.1	- .2	+ 5.9
A	- .7	- .1	- .8	+ 3.7	- 3.1	+ .6
S	- .6	- 2.0	- 2.6	+ 2.0	- 4.4	- 2.4
O	- 17.1	- 10.0	- 27.1	+ 15.4	- 14.2	+ 1.2
N	- 5.0	- 14.2	- 19.2	+ 13.6	- 42.1	- 28.5
D	- 32.5	+ 6.9	- 25.6	+ 2.1	+ 3.1	+ 5.2
Total	- 50.0	+ 27.0	- 23.0	+142.1	-121.7	+ 20.4
1923						
J	+ 17.8	- 21.8	- 4.0	+ 12.0	+ 4.3	+ 16.3
F	+ 2.7	+ 9.3	+ 12.0	+ 15.5	- 10.1	+ 5.4
M	+ 12.3	+ .9	+ 13.2	+ 8.4	+ 9.8	+ 18.2
A	+ .4	+ 2.8	+ 3.2	+ 2.7	+ 17.3	+ 20.0
M	+ 1.1	+ 11.1	+ 12.2	+ 1.0	+ 9.7	+ 10.7
J	+ 6.8	- .6	+ 6.2	+ 5.2	- 9.9	- 4.7
J	+ .8	+ 9.1	+ 9.9	+ 4.7	- 10.7	- 6.0
A	+ 13.7	- 5.4	+ 8.3	+ .6	- 3.4	- 2.8
S	+ 4.3	+ 4.8	+ 9.1	+ .2	+ 2.2	+ 2.4
O	- 2.8	- 9.9	- 12.7	+ 2.9	- 2.7	+ .2
N	+ 14.7	- 15.1	- .4	+ 3.4	- 63.2	- 59.8
D	- 4.0	+ 2.1	- 1.9	+ .9	- 38.2	- 37.3
Total	+ 67.8	- 12.7	+ 55.1	+ 57.5	- 94.9	- 37.4

TABLE VIII (cont' d)

Month	Balancing items			Long-term capital		
	MG	SC	T	fUS	AO	T
1924						
J	+ 10.9	- 5.8	+ 5.1	+ 11.4	- 12.6	- 1.2
F	+ 1.3	+ 2.5	+ 3.8	+ 12.0	- 13.7	- 1.7
M	+ 3.5	+ 12.8	+ 16.3	+ .9	- 5.1	- 4.2
A	+ 1.9	+ 4.8	+ 6.7	+ .9	+ 5.0	+ 5.9
M	+ .6	- 4.7	- 4.1	+ .6	- 20.0	- 19.4
J	+ .3	+ 2.0	+ 2.3	+ 1.9	- 17.2	- 15.3
J	- .6	+ 2.7	+ 2.1	+ 29.2	- 39.9	- 10.7
A	...	- 4.3	- 4.3	+ 31.6	- 36.6	- 5.0
S	- .9	+ 40.9	+ 40.0	+ 60.2	-113.3	- 53.1
O	- 25.7	- 31.1	- 56.8	+ 68.3	- 28.3	+ 30.0
N	- 14.5	- 21.2	- 35.7	+ 6.7	- 19.2	- 12.5
D	+ 1.9	- 14.3	- 12.4	+ 5.1	- 39.7	- 34.6
Total	- 21.3	- 15.7	- 37.0	+218.8	-340.6	-121.8
1925						
J	+ 7.4	- 14.4	- 7.0	+ 5.5	- 9.1	- 3.6
F	+ 6.6	+ 9.7	+ 16.3	+ 21.5	- 38.6	- 17.1
M	+ 5.0	+ 3.8	+ 8.8	+ 20.9	- 21.2	- .3
A	+ 3.4	- 17.4	- 14.0	+ 18.1	- 4.2	+ 13.9
M	- 1.4	+ 17.2	+ 15.8	+ 19.2	- 45.1	- 25.9
J	- .1	+ .6	+ .5	+ 10.5	- 20.0	- 9.5
J	+ .1	- 26.8	- 26.7	+ 6.4	+ 5.8	+ 12.2
A	...	- 8.0	- 8.0	+ 1.7	- 21.0	- 19.3
S	+ 15.0	- 28.6	- 13.6	+ 3.4	- 15.6	- 12.2
O	- 21.8	+ 15.0	- 6.8	+ 6.0	- 53.2	- 47.2
N	- 24.5	- 6.9	- 31.4	+ 3.5	- 31.6	- 28.1
D	- 1.3	- 37.0	- 38.3	+ 10.5	- 53.8	- 43.3
Total	- 11.6	- 92.8	-104.4	+127.2	-307.6	-180.4

TABLE VIII (cont'd)

Month	Balancing items			Long-term capital		
	MG	SC	T	fUS	AO	T
1926						
J	+ 10.6	- 78.8	- 68.2	+ 17.8	+ 49.7	+ 67.5
F	+ 11.5	+ 12.9	+ 24.4	+ 8.6	- 35.8	- 27.2
M	+ 44.1	+ 3.7	+ 47.8	+ 7.3	- 37.7	- 30.4
A	- 7.5	+ 31.5	+ 24.0	+ 21.5	- 35.9	- 14.4
M	- 21.6	+ 13.8	- 7.8	+ 28.6	- 13.9	+ 14.7
J	- 2.2	- 1.1	- 3.3	+ 24.3	- 40.0	- 15.7
J	- 2.3	- 3.0	- 5.3	+ 29.7	- 47.3	- 17.6
A	- 11.6	- 22.0	- 33.6	+ 20.0	+ 4.0	+ 24.0
S	- 2.7	- 12.0	- 14.7	+ 19.8	- 8.6	+ 11.2
O	- 3.2	- 7.8	- 11.0	+ 19.8	- 34.8	- 15.0
N	- 5.6	+ 20.2	+ 14.6	+ 3.2	- 67.3	- 64.1
D	- 8.5	- 9.2	- 17.7	+ 1.8	- 11.0	- 9.2
Total	+ 1.0	- 51.8	- 50.8	+202.4	-278.6	- 76.2
1927						
J	+ 34.2	- 4.9	+ 29.3	+ 9.5	- 30.6	- 21.1
F	- .5	- 13.5	- 14.0	+ 10.5	+ 14.7	+ 25.2
M	+ 1.8	+ 19.3	+ 21.1	+ 4.8	+ 4.0	+ 8.8
A	- 5.4	+ 28.5	+ 23.1	+ 29.6	- 50.0	- 20.4
M	- 3.6	+ 2.6	- 1.0	+ 37.1	- 38.7	- 1.6
J	- 2.0	- .5	- 2.5	+ 32.8	- 25.9	+ 6.9
J	+ .6	- 6.0	- 5.4	+ 22.1	- 5.4	+ 16.7
A	- 1.0	- 3.9	- 4.9	+ 1.0	- .8	+ .2
S	- 2.6	- 3.3	- 5.9	+ 34.4	- 31.7	+ 2.7
O	- 2.6	+ 8.5	+ 5.9	+ 51.6	- 49.9	+ 1.7
N	- 3.6	+ 11.9	+ 8.3	+ 26.8	- 74.5	- 47.7
D	- 22.3	- 22.7	- 45.0	+ 19.1	+ 10.5	+ 29.6
Total	- 7.0	+ 16.0	+ 9.0	+279.3	-278.3	+ 1.0

TABLE VIII (cont'd)

Month	Balancing items				Long-term capital		
	MG	SC	T		fUS	AO	T
1928							
J	+ 41.0	+ 39.9	+ 80.9		+ 20.7	- 94.4	- 73.7
F	+ 5.5	+ 3.3	+ 8.8		+ 15.2	- 9.3	+ 5.9
M	- 2.1	- 7.7	- 9.8		+ 5.7	+ 44.3	+ 50.0
A	- 1.9	+ 32.8	+ 30.9		+ 4.8	- 6.4	- 1.6
M	- 2.3	+ 8.6	+ 6.3		+ 35.6	- 30.7	+ 4.9
J	+ 9.9	- 10.4	- .5		+ 46.5	- 31.7	+ 14.8
J	+ 13.6	- 19.8	- 6.2		+ 16.0	- 31.8	- 15.8
A	- 2.0	- 5.7	- 7.7		+ 1.6	- .9	+ .7
S	- 4.9	+ 5.2	+ .3		+ 3.6	- 3.1	+ .5
O	- 2.0	+ 2.0	...		+ 11.7	- 20.1	- 8.4
N	- 2.5	+ 51.8	+ 49.3		+ 11.0	-106.4	- 95.4
D	- 3.3	- 13.0	- 16.3		+ 24.2	- 10.1	+ 14.1
Total	+ 49.0	+ 87.0	+136.0		+196.6	-300.6	-104.0
1929							
J	+ 35.6	- 34.7	+ .9		+ 29.4	- 9.0	+ 20.4
F	+ .3	+ 25.1	+ 25.4		+ 17.2	- 9.3	+ 7.9
M	+ .8	+ 5.5	+ 6.3		+ 29.4	+ 13.3	+ 42.7
A	- .6	+ 21.0	+ 20.4		+ 27.8	- 2.4	+ 25.4
M	- .3	- 9.5	- 9.8		+ 27.1	+ 19.4	+ 46.5
J	+ 2.1	+ 8.8	+ 10.9		+ 73.1	- 72.7	+ .4
J	- .2	- 31.4	- 31.6		+ 65.2	- 21.9	+ 43.3
A	- .4	+ 49.7	+ 49.3		+ 12.0	- 56.9	- 44.9
S	- .3	+ 35.9	+ 35.6		...	- 18.7	- 18.7
O	...	+ 28.8	+ 28.8		+ 20.4	- 28.1	- 7.7
N	...	+ 18.4	+ 18.4		+ 24.5	- 20.9	+ 3.6
D	...	- 29.6	- 29.6		+ 25.0	+ 42.1	+ 67.1
Total	+ 37.0	+ 88.0	+125.0		+351.1	-165.1	+186.0

TABLE VIII (cont'd)

Month	Balancing items			Long-term capital		
	MG	SC	T	fUS	AO	T
1930						
J	- .2	- 5.2	- 5.4	+ 30.5	+ 5.1	+ 35.6
F	- .1	- 6.5	- 6.6	+ 32.2	+ 10.8	+ 43.0
M	- .1	- 7.8	- 7.9	+ 26.9	+ 31.0	+ 57.9
A	- .8	+ 51.3	+ 50.5	+ 13.1	- 25.6	- 12.5
M	- .8	- 17.7	- 18.5	+ 25.9	+ 36.3	+ 62.2
J	- .7	- 11.2	- 11.9	+ 44.8	- 6.3	+ 38.5
J	- 1.7	- 25.5	- 27.2	+ 40.9	- 2.9	+ 38.0
A	- 16.7	- 14.1	- 30.8	+ 31.4	- .3	+ 31.1
S	- 9.3	+ 5.3	- 4.0	+ 19.5	- .6	+ 18.9
O	- 4.0	- 19.1	- 23.1	+ 48.5	- 5.1	+ 43.4
N	- 11.6	+ 24.5	+ 12.9	+ 49.4	- 34.0	+ 15.4
D	+ 10.0	+ 26.0	+ 36.0	+ 11.5	- 10.0	+ 1.5
Total	- 36.0	0.0	- 36.0	+374.6	- 1.6	+373.0
1931						
J	+ 22.4	- 13.3	+ 9.1	+ 48.6	- 37.6	+ 11.0
F	- 2.2	- 38.0	- 40.2	+ 41.0	+ 22.9	+ 63.9
M	- 2.6	+ 3.3	+ .7	+ 8.4	+ 29.8	+ 38.2
A	- 3.0	+ 57.3	+ 54.3	+ 14.7	- 35.5	- 20.8
M	- 2.7	+ 21.1	+ 18.4	+ 13.3	- 2.9	+ 10.4
J	+ 15.1	- 21.1	- 6.0	+ 6.5	+ 7.2	+ 13.7
J	- .3	+ 7.5	+ 7.2	+ 1.7	- 10.4	- 8.7
A	- 1.7	+ 2.1	+ .4	...	- 12.1	- 12.1
S	+ .6	+ 2.3	+ 2.9	+ 24.7	- 30.6	- 5.9
O	...	+ 13.5	+ 13.5	+ 26.7	- 37.0	- 10.3
N	+ 1.2	- 2.9	- 1.7	...	+ 9.6	+ 9.6
D	+ 6.2	- 3.8	+ 2.4	...	+ 24.0	+ 24.0
Total	+ 33.0	+ 28.0	+ 61.0	+185.6	- 72.6	+113.0

TABLE VIII (cont' d)

Month	Balancing items			Long-term capital		
	MG	SC	T	fUS	AO	T
1932						
J	+ 2.0	+ 23.3	+ 25.3	...	- 16.4	- 16.4
F	+ 2.9	+ 8.2	+ 11.1	...	+ 0.4	+ 0.4
M	+ 2.2	+ 6.1	+ 8.3	...	+ 22.7	+ 22.7
A	+ 2.2	+ 1.1	+ 3.3	...	+ 14.9	+ 14.9
M	...	+ 5.1	+ 5.1	...	+ 10.5	+ 10.5
J	+ 0.2	- 1.7	- 1.5	...	+ 8.7	+ 8.7
J	+ 0.9	- 3.2	- 2.3	...	- 1.4	- 1.4
A	- 1.2	- 14.1	- 15.3	+ 1.1	+ 2.1	+ 3.2
S	- 1.3	+ 11.0	+ 9.7	+ 11.6	- 27.4	- 15.8
O	- 2.7	+ 0.9	- 1.8	+ 12.5	- 10.9	+ 1.6
N	- 2.6	- 18.1	- 20.7	+ 2.2	+ 25.0	+ 27.2
D	+ 0.7	+ 19.4	+ 19.8	...	- 0.6	- 0.6
Total	+ 3.0	+ 38.0	+ 41.0	+ 27.4	+ 27.6	+ 55.0

TABLE IX

Canadian Monthly Short-and Long-Term Capital Accounts, 1933-34

(in millions of dollars)

| | Monetary gold | Balancing items | | Long-term capital | | | | |
| | | Short-term capital | Total | Outstanding Securities | | | Remaining movements | Total |
				Sales	Purchases	Total		
1933								
J	...	+ 9.3	+ 9.3	12.7	7.4	+ 5.3	- 10.7	- 5.4
F	...	- 8.0	- 8.0	13.9	16.0	- 2.1	+ 20.6	+ 18.5
M	+ 2.4	- 2.0	+ 0.4	7.5	7.5	...	+ 12.6	+ 12.6
A	- 2.5	- 4.3	- 6.8	17.1	11.6	+ 5.5	+ 12.6	+ 18.1
M	+ 2.7	- 2.9	- 0.2	22.5	13.7	+ 8.8	- 12.6	- 3.8
J	+ 3.4	+ 4.0	+ 7.4	33.4	20.9	+ 12.5	- 23.0	- 10.5
J	...	- 18.7	- 18.7	47.1	28.9	+ 18.2	- 13.0	+ 5.2
A	...	- 7.2	- 7.2	23.9	15.6	+ 8.3	- 10.6	- 2.3
S	...	- 22.3	- 22.3	23.0	24.9	- 1.9	+ 6.8	+ 4.9
O	...	+ 9.8	+ 9.8	31.0	29.8	+ 1.2	- 15.5	- 14.3
N	...	+ 43.3	+ 43.3	36.8	38.5	- 1.7	- 45.1	- 46.8
D	...	+ 23.0	+ 23.0	19.8	22.9	- 3.1	- 1.1	- 4.2
Total	+ 6.0	+ 24.0	+ 30.0	288.7	237.7	+ 51.0	- 79.0	- 28.0

TABLE IX (cont' d)

1934	Monetary gold	Balancing items Short-term capital	Total	Long-term capital — Outstanding Securities Sales	Purchases	Total	Remaining movements	Total
J	...	+ 4.5	+ 4.5	31.2	27.7	+ 3.5	- 16.1	- 12.6
F	- 2.5	- 13.7	- 16.2	29.2	27.4	+ 1.8	+ 9.5	+ 11.3
M	...	- 2.3	- 2.3	34.0	26.2	+ 7.8	- 4.2	+ 3.6
A	...	- 8.5	- 8.5	30.8	21.1	+ 9.7	+ 6.9	+ 16.6
M	...	- 12.4	- 12.4	25.2	24.7	+ 0.5	+ 14.3	+ 14.8
J	- 1.5	- 6.4	- 7.9	28.0	19.8	+ 8.2	- 8.0	+ 0.2
I	...	+ 12.6	+ 12.6	21.2	21.1	+ 0.1	- 27.1	- 27.0
A	...	- 10.7	- 10.7	29.2	35.9	- 6.7	- 5.3	- 12.0
S	...	+ 3.0	+ 3.0	19.1	27.8	- 8.7	- 7.6	- 16.3
O	...	+ 3.2	+ 3.9	26.8	26.3	+ 0.5	- 14.5	- 14.0
N	...	- 4.1	- 4.1	24.9	22.5	+ 2.4	- 1.5	+ 0.9
D	...	+ 15.1	+ 15.1	21.6	31.8	- 10.2	- 0.3	- 10.5
Total	- 4.0	- 19.0	- 23.0	321.2	312.3	+ 8.9	- 53.9	- 45.0

APPENDIX B

" PROPENSITIES " TO IMPORT CONSUMERS' AND PRODUCERS' GOODS

IMPORTS of consumers' goods on a fiscal year basis have been estimated by adding the multifarious items included in the two Department of Trade and Commerce categories "foods, beverages and smokers' supplies" and "personal and household utilities" as listed in the Canada Year Book. [1] Imports of producers' goods on a fiscal year basis have been obtained by adding the various items listed under imports of "producers' materials" and of "producers' equipment." [2] These were converted to a calendar year basis. To obtain consumers' and producers' goods imports for the calendar year 1926, for example one-quarter of the 1926 fiscal year figure has been added to three-quarters of the 1927 fiscal year figure. Each of these two calendar year series has then been increased by the percentage difference between their sum and total merchandise imports as estimated for balance of payments purposes.

Freight services were distributed between the two categories according to the percentage that each of the adjusted import figures formed of total trade imports. Tourist and travel payments were arbitrarily allocated wholly to the consumption sector. [3]

The corresponding marginal and average "propensities" to import with reference to current GNP are given in Table X. These calculations obviously can claim no great merit on the grounds of statistical purity. They are made merely to obtain a rough indication of the relationship between the flow of imported consumers' and producers' goods and their domestic counter-parts.

TABLE   X

"Propensities" to Import Consumers' and
Producers' Goods

	Consumers' goods and services		Producers' goods	
	Average	marginal	Average	marginal
1920	10.4		20.8	
1921	9.0	.16	14.6	.45
1922	7.6	...	12.8	...
1923	8.3	.21	14.9	.61
1924	7.8	...	12.9	...
1925	7.4	.04	13.5	.19
1926	8.2	.22	14.0	.24
1927	8.5	.16	14.2	.17
1926 (a)	8.2		14.0	
1927	8.4	.12	14.0	.13
1928	8.3	.07	15.0	.27
1929	8.8	.57	15.7	.85
1930	8.1	.16	13.0	.40
1931	6.7	.15	9.3	.30
1932	5.6	.12	8.0	.16
1933	5.1	.14	8.4	.03
1934	5.5	08	9.7	.20

(a)   The remaining "propensities" are calculated with reference to the revised
      (1952) D.B.S. estimates of current GNP.

APPENDIX C

TABLES

TABLE XI

Canada's International Accounts, 1919-35 (a)

(millions of dollars)

Year	Commodity trade			Tourist trade (b)		
	Exports	Imports	Balance (I-II)	Receipts	Payments	Balance (IV-V)
	I	II	III	IV	V	VI
1919	1,261.7	951.4	+ 310.3	75.9	52.4	+ 23.5
1920	1,267.1	1,428.7	- 161.6	91.4	62.5	+ 28.9
1921	800.4	827.8	- 27.4	98.2	57.5	+ 40.7
1922	884.1	744.6	+ 139.5	110.5	56.8	+ 53.7
1923	1,003.9	885.1	+ 118.8	130.7	61.8	+ 68.9
1924	1,032.6	789.9	+ 242.7	149.4	68.3	+ 81.1
1925	1,241.1	872.4	+ 368.7	170.4	69.7	+100.7
1926	1,272	973	+ 299	152	99	+ 53
1927	1,215	1,057	+ 158	163	100	+ 63
1928	1,341	1,209	+ 132	177	98	+ 79
1929	1,178	1,272	- 94	198	108	+ 90
1930	880	973	- 93	180	92	+ 88
1931	601	580	+ 21	153	71	+ 82
1932	495	398	+ 97	114	49	+ 65
1933	532	368	+ 164	89	44	+ 45
1934	648	484	+ 164	106	50	+ 56
1935	732	526	+ 206	117	64	+ 53

(a)   For sources, see above, chap. II, n. 6.

(b)   The tourist series for the period 1919-25 are not directly comparable with those for later years. The latter figures embody drastic revisions made on the basis of more accurate information obtained by field study during wartime exchange controls.

TABLE XI (cont'd)

Year	Interest and dividends			Freight and shipping		
	Receipts	Payments	Balance (VII-VIII)	Receipts	Payments	Balance (X-XI)
	VII	VIII	IX	X	XI	XII
1919	39.6	211.5	- 171.9	86.9	125.6	- 38.7
1920	46.8	212.9	- 166.1	114.4	170.1	- 55.7
1921	47.3	234.3	- 187.0	84.3	116.5	- 32.2
1922	39.9	230.3	- 190.4	78.5	94.3	- 15.8
1923	40.5	254.0	- 213.5	89.2	121.4	- 32.2
1924	40.3	242.3	- 202.0	83.0	99.1	- 16.1
1925	40.2	250.7	- 210.5	86.7	106.4	- 19.7
1926	32	240	- 208	96	105	- 9
1927	41	257	- 216	97	109	- 12
1928	46	275	- 229	96	116	- 20
1929	61	322	- 261	92	130	- 38
1930	59	348	- 289	70	103	- 33
1931	48	330	- 282	54	79	- 25
1932	37	302	- 265	38	66	- 28
1933	38	264	- 226	44	66	- 22
1934	57	268	- 211	52	79	- 27
1935	64	270	- 206	68	82	- 14

TABLE XI (cont' d)

Year	Non monetary gold exports	Other current items (a)			Total of all current items		
		Receipts	Payments	Balance (XIV - XV)	Receipts (I+IV+VII +X+XIII+ XIV)	Payments (II+ V+ VII+XI+ XV)	Balance (III+ VI+ IX+XII+ XIII+XVI)
	XIII	XIV	XV	XVI	XVII	XVIII	XIX
1919	5.0	35.1	121.9	- 86.8	1,504.2	1,462.8	+ 41.4
1920	4.6	45.5	49.4	- 3.9	1,569.8	1,923.6	- 353.8
1921	2.5	40.4	33.7	+ 6.7	1,073.1	1,269.8	- 196.7
1922	4.0	38.4	26.8	+ 11.6	1,155.4	1,152.8	+ 2.6
1923	12.5	46.1	18.3	+ 27.8	1,322.9	1,340.6	- 17.7
1924	28.3	48.3	23.5	+ 24.8	1,381.9	1,223.1	+ 158.8
1925	31.5	53.5	39.4	+ 14.1	1,623.4	1,338.6	+ 284.8
1926	30	83	121	- 38	1,665	1,538	+ 127
1927	32	85	120	- 35	1,633	1,643	- 10
1928	40	88	122	- 34	1,788	1,820	- 32
1929	37	80	125	- 45	1,646	1,957	- 311
1930	39	69	118	- 49	1,297	1,634	- 337
1931	57	59	86	- 27	972	1,146	- 174
1932	70	54	89	- 35	808	904	- 96
1933	82	44	89	- 45	829	831	- 2
1934	114	43	71	- 28	1,020	952	+ 68
1935	119	45	78	- 33	1,145	1,020	+ 125

(a) This item includes such entries as charitable and missionary contributions, advertising transactions, motion picture and entertainment royalties.

TABLE XI (cont' d)

Capital imports and exports arising from

Year	Changes in British and foreign holdings of Canadian securities			Net sales of out- standing securities	Net direct investment trans- actions	Insurance trans- actions balance (a)
	New issues	Maturities redemptions etc	Balance (XX-XXI)			
	XX	XXI	XXII	XXIII	XXIV	XXV
1919	239.4	216.2	+ 25.1	- 40		+ 30.9
1920	221.5	61.0	+ 153.7	- 55		+ 13.5
1921	246.3	113.9	+ 123.6	- 40		+ 26.1
1922	292.6	80.4	+ 210.3	- 20		- .01
1923	156.3	51.0	+ 109.6	- - 40		+ 9.0
1924	280.6	146.2	+ 143.0	- 50		- 0.4
1925	239.8	231.4	+ 13.0	- 80		+ 14.6
1926	326.2	165.9	+ 161	- 135		+ 26.3
1927	301.0	160.0	+ 141	- 171	+ 35	- 15
1928	207.0	200.0	+ 7	- 126	+ 21	- 12
1929	297.0	150.0	+ 147	- 2	+ 18	+ 19
1930	400.0	110.0	+ 290	+ 56	+ 37	+ 9
1931	200	202	- 2	+ 45	+ 10	+ 34
1932	104	105	- 1	+ 85	- 28	- 1
1933	134	166	- 32	+ 51	- 59	- 1
1934	111	169	- 58	+ 9	- 45	+ 3
1935	117	256	- 139	+ 51	- 44	- 18

(a) Prior to 1927 most of the allowance for insurance transactions was included in columns XIV and XV.

TABLE XI (cont'd)

Year	Capital imports and exports arising from		Net changes in bank balances abroad	Mone-tary gold move-ments (net)	Net Movement of balancing items (XXVIII+ XXIX)	Residual item (a) - (XIX+ XXVII+ XXX)
	Dominion government war finance dealings	Total net long-term capital (XXII+ XXIII+ XXIV+XXV+ XXVI)				
	XXVI	XXVII	XXVIII	XXIX	XXX	XXXI
1919	- 25.6	- 9.6	- 21.7	+ 8.9	- 12.8	- 19.0
1920	+ 31.0	+ 143.2	+ 42.4	+ 30.4	+ 72.8	+ 137.8
1921	+ 27.9	+ 137.6	+ 144.4	+ 39.5	+ 183.9	- 124.8
1922	+ 46.8	+ 237.1	+ 27.0	- 50.0	- 23.0	- 216.7
1923	+ 63.8	+ 142.4	- 12.7	+ 67.8	+ 55.1	- 179.8
1924	+ 20.7	+ 113.3	- 15.7	- 21.3	- 37.0	- 235.1
1925	+ 1.9	- 50.5	- 92.8	- 11.6	- 104.4	- 129.9
1926	+ 2.3	+ 54.6	- 51.8	+ 1	- 50.8	- 130.8
1927	+ 11.0	+ 1.0	+ 16.0	- 7	+ 9.0	...
1928	+ 6.0	- 104.0	+ 87.0	+ 49	+ 136.0	...
1929	+ 4.0	+ 186.0	+ 88.0	+ 37	+ 125.0	...
1930	- 19.0	+ 373.0	...	- 36	- 36.0	...
1931	+ 26	+ 113	+ 28	+ 33	+ 61	...
1932	...	+ 55	+ 38	+ 3	+ 41	...
1933	...	- 41	+ 24	+ 6	+ 30	+ 13
1934	...	- 91	- 19	- 4	- 23	+ 46
1935	...	- 150	...	- 2	- 2	+ 27

(a) Amount required to balance because of errors and omissions. In the years 1927-32 errors and omissions are reflected in column XXIII.

TABLE XII

Percentage Changes in Some Indicators of Business Activity, Canada, United Kingdom, and United States, 1921-2, 1929-30, 1929-33, 1933-4 (a)

Series	1921-2 Canada	1921-2 U.K.	1921-2 U.S.	1929-30 Canada	1929-30 U.K.	1929-30 U.S.	1929-33 Canada	1929-33 U.K.	1929-33 U.S.	1933-4 Canada	1933-4 U.K.	1933-4 U.S.
1. National income	4.7	-13.5	2.2	-10.6	- 2.9	-11.4	-48.8	-10.0	-51.6	18.1	5.1	17.3
2. Real national income	14.3	6.8	7.6	- 9.9	- 2.9	- 8.3	-34.0	+ 6.4	-34.9	16.7	3.9	9.5
3. Gross national product	3.6	...	1.5	-10.1	...	-10.6	-42.4	...	-49.3	13.6	...	16.1
4. Industrial production	27.3	19.7	26.9	-15.2	-10.9	-19.3	-39.6	-18.3	-36.1	21.8	8.7	3.9
5. Mineral production	20.6	52.8	5.7	- 5.5	- 5.4	-13.9	-10.2	-13.2	-28.7	21.3	0.0	4.9
6. Electric power	24.2	- 9.0	16.2	0.7	11.6	- 1.5	- 3.4	+45.4	-12.3	22.0	14.1	6.6
7. Carloadings	18.9	...	9.0	-11.3	...	-14.0	-42.5	...	-45.8	14.5	...	6.9
8. Farm production	17.9	...	10.8	- 7.2	...	- 1.0	- 2.8	...	- 4.0	1.5	...	3.1
9. Construction	32.0	10.1	41.1	-21.0	2.1	-21.4	-82.7	+14.5	-78.6	26.0	14.2	28.0
10. Residential	35.9	...	54.5	-27.6	5.7	-42.5	-81.5	+40.8	-87.4	12.8	11.7	9.1
11. Non-residential	39.3	...	35.4	-18.8	- 3.4	-12.0	-83.6	-25.9	-73.9	29.7	21.5	29.7
12. Manufacturing	25.3	24.6	28.4	+16.7	- 5.0	-20.2	-32.1	-24.8	-37.0	16.9	10.4	4.0
13. Consumers' goods	13.8	22.7	24.2	- 6.5	- 1.0	-13.2	-15.7	-10.0	-24.5	9.0	- 6.2	9.4
14. Producers' goods	24.7	26.7	35.2	-17.4	- 8.5	-22.6	-52.5	-29.9	-43.8	27.6	32.0	- 0.4
15. Employment	0.2	3.3	10.6	- 4.7	- 6.4	-12.8	-29.9	-10.6	-30.8	15.1	4.0	16.8
16. Wholesale prices	-11.5	-19.5	- 0.9	- 9.4	-12.5	- 9.3	-29.8	-26.1	-30.7	6.7	3.2	13.6

(a) The change in the second year as a percentage of the figure for the first year. Canadian sources: for rows 1, 2 and 3 see chap. II n. 1 and n. 2; for remainder see Appendix D. United Kingdom sources: see Appendix D. United Kingdom coal production is used for row 5. United States sources: see Appendix D.

TABLE XIII

Sequence of Major Cyclical Peaks and Troughs in Canada's Exports, 1921,
1929, and 1933. (a)

V = Vegetable products, A = Animal products, F = Farming products (i.e. V+A),
NF = Non-farming products, NFM = Non-ferrous metals and their products,
W = Wood and its products, C = Chemicals and their products, I = Iron and its
products, FI = Fibres and their products, NMM = Non-metallic minerals and products,
M = Miscellaneous products, T = Total exports.

	To all countries	To U.K.	To U.S.	To other countries (b)
Troughs				
1921 Feb.				C
Apr.		T,F,V,C		
May	NFM	NFM	W	NFM
June	W			FI
July		I,FI	A,F	
Aug.	C			
Sept.	I		I,C,NFM	I
1922 Jan.	FI,NMN,NF		FI,V,NF	W,NF,(c)V,F,T
Feb.	M	W,M,NF	T	
Apr.	T,V,A,F			
May		A	NMM	A
June		NMM		
1923 Feb.			M	M,NMM
Peaks				
1928 July		A		
Sept.			A	
Oct.	A	W,I,NF		C, NMM
Nov.	V,F	T,V,F		T,V,F
Dec.				A
1929 Jan.		NMM		
Apr.	I		I	I
May	M	M		
June	FI		FI	
July			NFM	
Aug.	W			FI
Sept.			M	
Oct.	C,NMM,NF	C	W,NMM,NF	W,NFM,M,NF
Nov.		FI	T,V,F	
1930 Jan.	NFM		C	
May		NFM		

TABLE XIII (cont' d)

	To all countries	To U.K.	To U.S.	To other countries
Troughs				
1930 May		A		
1931 Jan.		T,V, FI, C,F		FI
Feb.		W		
Sept.		NMM		
Nov.			C	
Dec.	C (d)			I
1932 Feb.				C
Apr.				NMM
June		NFM		
July				W
Aug.			V	
Nov.			A,F	
1933 Jan.	NFM,FI	NF		
Feb	T,NF,V,W,I,		T,W,I,	
			NF,	T,NFM,NF
	NMM,M		FI,M	
Apr.	F,A		NFM,NMM	A
Dec.		I,M		
1934 Feb.·				F,V,M

(a) Since the method of adjusting trade figures used for balance of payments purposes to overcome the March-April distortion (see Appendix A) assumes that grain exports are a relatively large part of the total, it is not suitable for adjusting other component series. Hence, for comparability of all series in obtaining cyclical troughs and peaks, the values of March and April have been averaged. Source: Monthly Report of the Trade of Canada.

(b) Data on Other Countries derived by subtracting rounded data on the United Kingdom and the United States from the aggregate data rounded.

(c) Same value four months earlier.

(d) Lower value eleven months previous.

TABLE XIV
Growth in Some Sectors of the Economy (a)

Sector	Percentage change in index from		
	1920-3	1 923-9	1929-37
Automobile production	+ 56.3	+ 78.4	- 21.0
Newspring production	+ 42.8	+115.3	+ 34.8
Electric power	+ 37.6	+121.6	+ 54.1
Lead production	+ 30.9	+193.6	+ 26.1
Forestry	+ 27.8	+ 29.8	+ 23.2
Manufacturing production	+ 22.0	+ 36.3	+ 4.9
Industrial production	+ 19.9	+ 52.0	- 0.4
Iron and steel production	+ 16.4	+ 64.3	- 19.0
Construction	+ 13.6	+ 93.1	- 65.0
Mineral production	+ 12.2	+ 60.2	+ 54.0
Distribution	+ 0.7	+ 34.2	- 7.9

(a) Source: M.R.B.S. Peak years are compared to avoid the difficulty
of special behaviour of some series at various times during the cycle

TABLE XV

Velocity of Circulation of Active Bank Deposits,
Canada, 1919-24 (a)

Month	1919	1920	1921	1922	1923	1924
Jan.	2.22	3.04	3.27	3.25	3.29	2.98
Feb.	1.97	2.65	2.91	2.73	2.62	3.03
March	2.18	2.73	2.97	3.21	2.96	2.74
April	2.48	2.73	3.24	2.76	2.85	2.74
May	3.15	3.02	3.21	3.63	3.46	3.21
June	2.78	3.01	3.17	3.23	3.13	2.72
July	2.97	3.16	3.15	3.19	3.21	3.27
Aug.	2.83	2.94	2.99	2.99	3.11	2.81
Sept.	2.82	2.98	3.00	3.07	2.83	3.08
Oct.	3.23	3.59	3.29	3.32	4.17	3.45
Nov.	2.59	3.93	3.59	3.59	4.24	3.99
Dec.	3.10	3.87	3.60	3.60	3.39	3.65

(a) Bank Debits divided by Active Deposits. Bank Debits taken from
M.R.B.S., Supplement, May, 1934, Original Monthly Statistics of Chief
Economic Importance, 52. Active bank deposits have been defined to include
(1) Balances due Provincial and Dominion Governments, (2) Demand Deposits,
and (3) 10 per cent of Notice Deposits, all of which have been compiled from the
"Monthly Returns of the Chartered Banks."

TABLE XVI

Canadian Product-Wages and Unit Wage-cost

Year	Product wages (a) A (1913 = 100)	Product wages (b) B (1913 = 100)	Unit wage-cost (c) (1926 = 100)
1920	85.3	83.4	156.7
1921	110.5	113.0	165.9
1922	118.6	122.6	124.1
1923	120.4	124.5	110.9
1924	120.1	128.6	114.4
1925	115.5	123.4	104.6
1926	119.3		100.0
1927	124.8		98.3
1928	127.6		90.4
1929	131.3		88.6
1930	145.7		101.6
1931	167.9		112.4
1932	170.5		114.2
1933	160.6		97.4
1934	152.5		89.0
1935	155.8		86.7

(a)   Average weighted index of wage-rates divided by the wholesale price index.

(b)   Average weighted index of wage-rates divided by the domestic goods price index (Federal Reserve Bulletins).

(c)   The average yearly earnings of wage-earners in manufacturing industries (C.Y.B.,) converted to an index and then divided by the Index of manufacturing production. This index is somewhat lower than warranted in the 1925-30 period because of a change in the method of computing the number of employees which increased the apparent number.

TABLE XVII

Cash and Secondary Reserves of Canadian Banks (a)

(millions of dollars)

Date	Total public liabilities (c)	Cash reserve in Canada Amount (d)	% of Col. 2 (e)	Secondary reserves Amount (f)	% of Col. 2(e)
1930					
March	2297	162	7.1	199	8.7
June	2300	158	6.9	173	7.5
Sept.	2310	164	7.1	213	9.2
Dec.	2264	174	7.7	194	8.6
1931					
March	2253	148	6.6	241	10.7
June	2265	151	6.7	201	8.9
Sept.	2230	157	7.0	206	9.2
Dec.	2199	175	8.0	210	9.5
1932					
March	2129	158	7.4	173	8.1
June	2055	165	8.0	170	8.3
Sept.	2021	151	7.5	179	8.9
Dec.	2043	191	9.3	178	8.7
1933					
March	2013	178	8.8	176	8.7
June	2095	177	8.4	172	8.2
Sept.	2105	166	7.9	215	10.2
Dec.	2052	179	8.7	137	6.7

(a)   Source: "Monthly Returns of the Chartered Banks," Canada Gazette.
(b)   Last juridical day of the month.
(c)   Notes in circulation, notice deposits, demand deposits, and Dominion and provincial government deposits.
(d)   Specie and Dominion notes held in Canada.
(e)   Percentage of total public liabilities.
(f)   Specie held abroad and items listed in Appendix A, n. 24

APPENDIX D
STATISTICAL SOURCES

(Full publication details are not given for those authoities also listed in the
Bibliography. Nor is any reference made here to sources which have been given
in full in the text.)

OFFICIAL

Canada Gazette. Ottawa. Monthly Returns of the Chartered Banks, 1919-35.
    For monthly banking statistics.

Department of Trade and Commerce. Quarterly Report of the Trade of Canada
    (Monthly Report of the Trade of Canada from 1920 to March 1927). Ottawa,
    1920-38. For monthly merchandise exports and imports (by origin classification)
    to various geographical areas.

Dominion Bureau of Statistics. Canada Year Book. Ottawa, 1919-39. For wage-rate
    indexes, monthly and yearly indexes of retail sales, net value of production of
    manufacturing and other industries, wages and average yearly earnings in
    manufacturing, index of efficiency of production in manufacturing, yearly
    averages of banking statistics including reserve ratios, volume and value of
    wheat stocks and production, revenue and expenditure of governments, govern-
    ment indebtedness, population, national income and total income payments
    to individuals 1920-6, income produced by governments, and Dominion notes
    in circulation per capita.

------ Monthly Review of Business Statistics. Ottawa, various dates as follows:
    (i)   November 1931. Supplement, Twelve Years of the Economic Statistics
           of Canada by Months and Years, 1919-1930. For monthly indexes of
           preferred and common stock prices; new issues of bonds; number and
           liabilities of commercial failures; freight ton miles; passenger miles;
           railway operating revenue; index of over-all employment; percentage
           of unemployment in trade unions; Employment Office placements,
           applications, and vacancies; number of strikes; number of employees on
           strike; and days lost on strikes. (Compiled from successive issues of
           Prices and Price Indexes and M.R.B.S. for 1931-5.)

    (ii)   November 1932, Supplement, Monthly Indexes of the Physical Volume
           of Business in Canada. For monthly indexes of forestry, lead, coal,
           foodstuffs, pneumatic casings, boots and shoes, newsprint, iron and steel,
           steel imports, pig iron, automobile, coke, and electric power production;
           livestock, cattle, sheep and hog slaughterings; tobacco released for
           consumption; costs of construction; building permits; carloadings; volume

of imports and exports; employment in trade; shares traded in Montreal; livestock, agricultural, and grain marketings; wheat receipts, cattle, calf, and hog sales on stockyards; cold storage; and wholesale prices. (Compiled from successive issues of M.R.B.S. for the period after September 1932.)

(iii)   May 1934, Supplement, Original Monthly Statistics of Chief Economic Importance. For shares traded on the Toronto stock exchange and bank debits.

(iv)   June 1935, Supplement, Recent Economic Tendencies in Canada, 1919-1934. For annual price of London sterling in Montreal, United Kingdom coal and electricity production, index of United Kingdom industrial production, United States electrical production, yearly indexes of costs of construction and of the prices of common and preferred stocks and long-term interest rates (1931-4).

(v)   January 1938, Supplement, Economic Fluctuations in Canada during the Post-war Period. For annual indexes of carloadings; volume of agricultural, iron and steel, automobile, newsprint, lead, forestry, manufacturing, and electric power production; volume of imports and exports; and France's industrial production.

(vi)   February 1944. For indexes of physical volume of business; industrial, mineral and manufacturing production; construction; and distribution.

(vii)   July 1946. For construction contracts awarded (total and major components) and annual building permits issued.

(viii)   Successive issues. For monthly indexes of employment by industries (1929-35), stock prices, call loans, current loans, aggregate issues of Dominion notes, notes in the hands of the public, and demand deposits; and annual crop yield.

------ National Accounts, Income and Expenditure, 1926-1950. Ottawa, 1952. For revised national income, GNP, and investment data starting in 1926.

------ Prices and Price Indexes. Ottawa, successive issues. For indexes of cost of living, rent, and general wholesale prices; monthly indexes of Dominion of Canada long-term bond prices and yields; prices of wheat, cattle, and newsprint in Canada; indexes of prices of consumers' goods and producers' goods; monthly indexes of common and preferred stock prices after 1930; Bureau of Labor Statistics (United States) general wholesale price index; Board of Trade (United Kingdom) wholesale price index; annual price indexes of total exports and imports and of their main broad categories.

------ By correspondence with S. B. Smith. Monthly and annual yield of Dom-inion of Canada theoretical 15 year bond; monthly indexes of employ-ment by industries (1921-8), production of consumers' and of producers' goods, bank debits, and "economic conditions in Canada"; annual salaries and wages paid (in total and by major industrial sectors); corpor-ation profits; new bond issues by type of security and by country of place-ment (1933-5); and iron and steel and forestry production indexes (1933-5).

Federal Reserve Bulletin. Successive issues. For monthly yield of United States (government) long-term bonds; United States monthly wholesale price indexes until 1926; Canadian domestic prices (1920-5); average monthly price of the Canadian dollar in New York; and the following United States indexes: industrial, manufacturing, and mineral production, employment in manufacturing industries, freight carloadings, and construction contracts awarded (residential, non-residential, and total).

League of Nations, World Production and Prices, 1925-32. For indexes of United Kingdom production of producers' and consumers' goods (1929-33).

Statistical Abstract of the United States. Successive issues. For annual yield of United States (government) long-term bonds, public debt, population, and index of the volume of farm production.

UNOFFICIAL

Beveridge, W.H.   Full Employment in a Free Society. London: Allen & Unwin, 1944. For unemployment rate in Great Britain and Northern Ireland, index of "construction and instruments" production (used as a criterion of construction, 1921-9); total, dwelling houses, and other buildings plans approved (used as criteria of United Kingdom total, residential, and non-residential construction, 1929-34); indexes of production in general industry, the textile and the "construction and instrument" industries (used as criteria of manufacturing production, 1929-34, consumers' goods production, 1933-4, and producers' goods production, 1933-4).

Bowley. A.L.   Studies in the National Income 1924-1938. Cambridge: University Press, 1944. For United Kingdom cost of living index and national income (1924-38). (The latter has been deflated by the former to obtain United Kingdom real national income.)

Cowles, Alfred, 3rd, and Associates.   Common-stock Indexes 1871-1937.
    Bloomington: Principia Press, 1938. For monthly indexes of various
    United States common stock prices.

Hoffmann, Walther.   " Ein Index der industriellen Produktion für Gross-
    britannien seit dem Jahrhundert. " Weltwirtschaftliches Archiv, Band 40,
    Heft 2 (September 1934), 398. For indexes of production in all United
    Kingdom industries, consumers' goods and producers' goods industries
    (used as criteria of production in manufacturing, consumers' goods and pro-
    ducers' goods industries, 1920-31.)

Kuznets, S.   National Income and Its Composition, 1919-1938. New York:
    National Bureau of Economic Research, 1941. For United States money
    and real national income. •

------ Uses of National Income in Peace and War. New York: National Bureau
    of Economic Research, Occasional Paper 6, March 1942, 37. For United
    States gross national product.

Leong, Y.S.   " Indexes of the Physical Volume of Producers' Goods, Consumers'
    Goods, Durable Goods, and Transient Goods. " Journal of the American
    Statistical Association, vol. XXX, no. 190 (June 1935) 361-76. For
    yearly indexes of the United States production of producers' goods and
    consumers' goods (including automobiles), 1920-34.

Stone, Richard.   " The Analysis of Market Demand. "   Journal of the Royal
    Statistical Society, vol. CVIII (1945), 286-332. For United Kingdom
    real and money national income, 1919-24.

SELECTED BIBLIOGRAPHY

Angell, J.W.   The Theory of International Prices. Cambridge, 1926.

Beach, W. Edwards.   British International Gold Movements and Banking
    Policy, 1881-1913.   Cambridge, 1935.

Bloomfield, A.I.   "The Significance of Outstanding Securities in the International
    Movement of Capital." Canadian Journal of Economics and Political Science,
    VI, 4 (November 1940), 495-524.

Brown, A.J.   "Trade Balances and Exchange Stability." Oxford Economic Papers,
    6 (April 1942), 57-75.

Bryce, R.B.   " The Effects on Canada of Industrial Fluctuations in the United
    States." Canadian Journal of Economics and Political Science, V, 3
    (August 1939), 373-86.

Cairncross, A.   "Die Kapitaleinfuhr in Kanada, 1900-13."
    Weltwirtschaftliches Archiv (November 1937).

Chang, T.C.   "A Note on Exports and National Income in Canada." Canadian
    Journal of Economics and Political Science, XIII, 2 (May 1947), 276-80.

Curtis, C.A.   "The Canadian Monetary Situation." Journal of Political
    Economy, XL, 3 (June 1932), 314-37.

Elliott, G.A.   "Transfer of Means-of-Payment and the Terms of International
    Trade." Canadian Journal of Economics and Political Science, II, 4
    (November 1936), 481-92.

Hansen, A.H.   Monetary Theory and Fiscal Policy. New York, 1949.

Hawtrey, R.G.   Currency and Credit. London, 1927, 3rd ed.

Hicks, J.R.   A Contribution to the Theory of the Trade Cycle. Oxford, 1950.

Keynes, J.M.   The General Theory of Employment, Interest and Money,
    London, 1936.

Kindleberger, C.P.   International Short-term Capital Movements. New York,
    1937.

Knox, F.A.   Dominion Monetary Policy, 1929-1934. Ottawa: Royal Commission
    on Dominion-Provincial Relations, 1939.

Machlup. F.   International Trade and the National Income Multiplier.
    Philadelphia, 1943.

Mackintosh, W.A.   The Economic Background of Dominion-Provincial Relations.
    Ottawa, 1939.

Meade, J.E. and Andrews, P.W.S. " Summary of Replies to Questions on Effects
    of Interest Rates". Oxford Economic Papers, 1 (October 1938), 14-31.

Metzler, L.A. " Underemployment Equilibrium in International Trade."
    Econometrica, X (1942), 97-112.

Morgenstern, O. " On the International Spread of Business Cycle." Journal of
    Political Economy, LI, 4 (August 1943), 287-309.

Neisser, Hans. Some International Aspects of the Business Cycle. Philadelphia,
    1936.

Nurkse, R.   Internationale Kapitalbewegungen.   Wien, 1935.

Ohlin, B.   Interregional and International Trade.   Cambridge, 1933.

Parkinson, J.F.   Canadian Investment and Foreign Exchange Problems.
    Toronto, 1940.

Plumptre, A.F.W.   Central Banking in the British Dominions. Toronto, 1947.

Polak, J.J.   " The International Propagation of Business Cycles." Review of
    Economic Studies. VI, 2 (February 1939), 79-99.

Robbins, L.   The Great Depression. London, 1934.

Robertson, D.H.   "A Survey of Modern Monetary Controversy." Manchester
    School, IX (1938), 133-53.

Salant, W.A.   "Foreign Trade Policy in the Business Cycle." Public Policy, II,
    ed. C.J. Friedrich and E.S. Mason. Cambridge, Mass., 1941, 208-31.

Samuelson, P.A.   "A Synthesis of the Principle of Acceleration and the Multiplier."
    Journal of Political Economy, XLVII, 6 (December 1939), 786-97.

Sayers, R.S.   "Business Men and the Terms of Borrowing. " Oxford Economic
     Papers, 3 (February 1940), 23-31.

Timlin, Mabel F.   Keynesian Economics.   Toronto, 1942.

Tinbergen, J.   Statistical Testing of Business Cycle Theories, I, II. Geneva, 1939.

Viner, Jacob.   Canada's Balance of International Indebtedness, 1900-1913.
     Cambridge, 1924.

------ Studies in the Theory of International Trade. London, 1937.

FOOTNOTES

Chapter One

1. J. A. Schumpeter, Business Cycles: A Theoretical, Historical, and Statistical Analysis of the Capitalist Process, I (New York, 1939), 367. Tse Chun Chang has found a similar phenomenon for Britain in the inter-war period evidently by (i) equating the business cycle to fluctuations in income and (ii) using wholesale prices as a short-run index of income. "The British Balance of Payments, 1924-1938," Economic Journal, LVII, no. 228 (December, 1947), 482 n.

2. C. P. Kindleberger, International Short-term Capital Movements (New York, 1937), 141f. Cf. Chang, "The British Balance of Payments," 481f.

3. R. G. Hawtrey, Currency and Credit (3rd ed., London, 1927), 60.

4. Ibid., 152.

5. If a country has an inconvertible paper standard, it may enjoy expanding credit and rising prices while contraction becomes chronic in other countries. Still, it may receive contractive impulses from abroad since (i) the merchants whose forced sales are first induced by credit contraction in the gold standard countries (say) will trade not only in gold standard areas but also in the paper standard market -- at least until the paper currency actually depreciates; (ii) the eventual decrease of consumers' outlay in the gold standard countries may induce the paper standard country to quote lower prices instead of less favourable rates of exchange; and (iii) "if the credit system of a paper-using country is left entirely to itself, the outcome will probably be some sympathetic credit" movement combined with some movement of the foreign exchanges. Ibid., 140f. Thus sympathetic production, price and credit movements may be effected without gold flows.

6. See especially F. A. Hayek, Monetary Theory and the Trade Cycle (London, 1933) and Prices and Production (2nd rev. and enlarged ed., London, 1935).

7. Monetary Theory and the Trade Cycle, 179f.

8. Ragnar Nurkse, Internationale Kapitalbewegungen (Vienna, 1935).

9. Nurkse assumes a condition of full employment for the original starting-point when dealing with the effect of a capital import (ibid., 187); but he is not explicit whether he is similarly following Hayek in these later models.

10. Nurkse points out that under paper standard conditions such normal capital movements are not so frequent as irregular movements, capital flights, and speculative transactions (ibid., 211).

11. G. Cassel, The Theory of Social Economy, translation of 5th German ed. (New York, 1932), 642.

12. J. W. Angell, The Theory of International Prices (Cambridge, Mass., 1926), 527.

13. Ibid., 528.

14. J. Viner, Studies in the Theory of International Trade (London, 1937), 434-5.

15. Foster and Catchings stressed the pernicious effect of business savings because they appeared quantitatively more important.

16. Since many firms require a capital asset to pay for itself in five years or less because of the danger of obsolescence, the rate of interest is often of negligible influence in discounting future returns. A second factor minimizing the role of interest is the growing tendency of larger businesses to finance capital expenditure from undistributed profits and reserve funds, often without calculating the imputed interest. Interest is more important in the case of buildings, public utilities, and transportation equipment because (i) they are of a semi-permanent nature -- since the output from such investment is likely to extend far into the future, the discounted price of such output becomes extremely sensitive to interest changes; (ii) the risk of obsolescence is not large for such investment so that interest rate changes are not as likely to be cancelled by risk changes as with other types of investment; and (iii) public regulation of rates charged by public utilities and transportation companies often prevents the accumulation of funds for further investment.

17. I.e., planned, proposed, or scheduled savings and investment in contrast with the ex post (realized or completed) savings and investment which are always equal.
   If an instantaneous multiplier prevails and if the full effects of interest rate changes on investment are also instantaneous, then the equilibrium level of income and hence of savings will be attained immediately and the actual income path can be read off the IS curve. But in the real world lags prevail in the effects of both interest rate changes and the multiplier; hence a period elapses before the attainment of equilibrium levels of income and savings, during which time the actual income level will not lie on the IS curve.

18. The shape of the IS curve would be much the same if the commodity price level were substituted for national income on the horizontal axis. Cf. J. R. Hicks, "Mr. Keynes and the 'Classics': A Suggested Interpretation," Econometrica, V, no. 2 (April, 1937), 158.

19. This useful formulation of the Keynesian theory was first presented by Hicks, ibid., 147-59.
   The fact that LS expresses income as a function of the interest rate and LM expresses the interest rate as a function of income causes no difficulty. With any

two functional relationships, $x = f(y)$ and $y = g(x)$, the point of intersection still yields the consistent solution or equilibrium position.

20. Hicks has shown that lags in this mechanism may, along the lines of the "cobweb theorem," give rise to a monetary cycle theory. Hicks, A Contribution to the Theory of the Trade Cycle (Oxford, 1950), chap. XI.

21. It must be noted that wherever the rate of increase of the physical output of consumers' goods falls because of shortages of particular factors of production rather than a diminution, relative or absolute, of consumption demand, such a sequence cannot be construed to fit an underconsumption theory.

22. P. A. Samuelson, "A Synthesis of the Principle of Acceleration and the Multiplier," Journal of Political Economy, XLVII, no. 6 (December, 1939), 786-97.

23. J. M. Keynes,   The General Theory of Employment, Interest and Money (London, 1936), 253f.

24. Monetary business cycle theories are exogenous in that the maximum quantity of bank credit can often be considered a datum in so far as there is a limit to gold reserves or bank cash. Exogenous theories emphasize changes in such data; endogenous theories emphasize the internal relationships (with or without lags) or the internal functioning of the economic system. See A. H. Hansen, Business Cycles and National Income (New York, 1951), 411ff.

25. Thus as far as the down-turn is concerned these three exogenous theories, (1) multiplier-accelerator, (2) multiplier-capital stock, and (3) shape of the consumption function, are diametrically opposed to a fourth exogenous theory, Cassel's, which stresses shortage of savings. (See Erik Lundberg, Studies in the Theory of Economic Expansion, Stockholm, 1937, 217-34, on how the Cassel-Spiethoff theory can be embodied in a model with oscillations.)

26. See F. Machlup, International Trade and the National Income Multiplier (Philadelphia, 1943).

27. An "induced" change in exports is one resulting from a change of income; "autonomous" changes in exports are not caused by (prior) income changes.

Chapter Two

1. Real net national income was obtained by deflating the current series (Dominion Bureau of Statistics, Canada Year Book, 1945, Ottawa, 1945, 905) by the cost of living index. (Henceforth Dominion Bureau of Statistics will be contracted to D.B.S. and the Canada Year Book to C.Y.B.)

2. Real GNP was obtained by deflating current GNP (D.B.S., Monthly Review of Business Statistics (henceforth contracted to M.R.B.S.), March, 1944, 15) by a composite price index derived by combining the D.B.S. price indexes of consumers' and producers' goods in the ratio 4 to 1. This ratio corresponds roughly with the comparative size of consumption and gross investment in the revised D.B.S. estimates for 1926.

On the inferior quality of the pre-1926 national accounts see D. C. MacGregor, "The Problem of Price Level in Canada," Canadian Journal of Economics and Political Science (henceforth contracted to C.J.E.P.S.), XIII, no. 2 (May, 1947), 181, 189. Even though these tentative estimates leave much to be desired from the standpoint of statistical purity, it seemed preferable to use them rather than to hazard guesses. Sufficient justification for this procedure is that the fluctuations of the old series are not radically divergent from those of the new series (D.B.S., National Accounts, Income and Expenditure, 1926-1950, Ottawa, 1952) for the remaining years under study. In fact so little difference was encountered, especially when both real series were used, that the substitution of the old for the new series in the post-1926 period would mean no significant change in the conclusions.

3. Difficulties arise as to an appropriate definition and also a statistical measure of the business cycle. No definition of the business cycle has as yet obtained general agreement among economists. Business cycles are believed by some to be departures from and returns to an economic equilibrium or normal state of trade. The mechanism by which such oscillations are effected is sometimes attached as a necessary attribute. According to Burns and Mitchell a cycle consists of expansions, recessions, contractions, and revivals occurring at about the same time in many economic activities (A. F. Burns and W. C. Mitchell, Measuring Business Cycles, New York, 1946, 3; see also Mitchell, Business Cycles: The Problem and Its Setting, New York, 1927, 468). Greater agreement might be reached perhaps on the proposition that fluctuations in general physical activity are involved. It seems preferable to take some such obvious characteristic of cyclical fluctuations as pointing to a provisional definition rather than equate the business cycle to its intricate or unseen generating forces. In this way an open mind may be kept as to the basic causal factors and it will not be necessary to conclude that business cycle was present if a certain set of forces was not the prime instigator in any particular case.

But no straightforward method of measuring the volume of business and industrial activity in real terms presents itself. For lack of suitable indexes, perhaps roughly concurrent fluctuations in many individual series may be used. Where the fluctuations in these individual series are not closely concurrent, resort must be made to a more debatable procedure, that of averaging the data to determine roughly the

approximate timing of the different phases of the business cycle. Choosing
"significant" series then poses a further problem.

Three criteria seem relevant. First, a series is more suitable the wider the
sector of the economy it measures. Where activities in various regions are highly
specialized and over-all series are inadequate, series representative of the various
economic regions must be considered. Secondly, selected series should preferably
be indexes of real activity rather than monetary magnitudes. Resort to series in
money terms may be appropriate when suitable volume indexes are not available,
providing major monetary disturbances are not prevalent. Thirdly, seasonally
adjusted series facilitate concentration on cyclical characteristics. Thus in averaging
such selected series perhaps more weight should be given to seasonally adjusted real
series representative of the economy as a whole.

Since homogeneous causes cannot be assumed to have been operating throughout
all the series studied, no great validity can be attached to the product obtained
from any such averaging process. (Cf. L. Robbins, An Essay on the Nature and
Significance of Economic Science, 2nd ed., London, 1946, 112f.) The result of
such methods is purely conventional. This procedure appears useful in empirical
study, however, for at least two reasons. First, the relative importance of a
specific factor in determining the level of economic activity in any one country can
be ascertained to a certain, if limited, extent by comparing its behaviour with that
of most other series. Thus, generally speaking, where a factor exhibits expansionary
forces appreciably later than most other factors, it may have contributed to the
upswing but not to the up-turn itself. Secondly, some indication of the relative
timing of economic activity in different countries is required. Usually for the
former reason, this averaging process is often undertaken in empirical analysis of
business cycles, although the limitations of the procedure are seldom made explicit.

4. To avoid the difficulty in selecting an item of the array as the median where
the array consists of an even number of items, the first item on the earlier (in time)
side of exact centre was chosen as the "median" rather than the later item. This
rule was followed consistently throughout the study.

5. This conclusion is conservative also in that some of the seasonally adjusted
volume indexes with troughs in 1922 may have been unduly influenced by strong
random factors, namely the Canadian and American coal strikes in 1922. Thus
the cyclical troughs in the coal, coke, pig iron, and steel production series may
have been earlier than the indexes indicate.

6. See Appendix C, Table XI. All annual international account estimates
for 1919 to 1925 and the 1926 capital account are from F. A. Knox, Dominion
Monetary Policy, 1929-1934 (Ottawa: Royal Commission on Dominion-Provincial
Relations, 1939), 89-93, except for the monetary gold and for freight and shipping
which are from Knox's Excursus, "Canadian Capital Movements and the Canadian
Balance of International Payments, 1900-1934" in H. Marshall, F. A. Southard, Jr.,
and K. W. Taylor, Canadian-American Industry (New Haven, 1936), 314f;

estimates for the other years are taken from D.B.S., The Canadian Balance of
International Payments, Preliminary Statement, 1946 (Ottawa, 1947).

    7. See Appendix A for the procedure used in estimating the monthly inter-
national accounts and for the data.

    8. A trough sometime in 1922 or later seems probable for both interest and
dividend receipts and "all other current credits" since they had lower annual totals
in 1922 than 1921.

    9. The low value in July 1921 of the seasonally adjusted index of export volume
can be selected as the trough of this index since it is surrounded by similarly low
values; the lower index in April 1922 has relatively high neighbouring values.

    10. The relatively sharp fall of total imports could only have been a minor
factor. A minor expansionary effect might have occurred in so far as a decreased
volume of foreign commodities and services were exchanged against Canadian
incomes which had not decreased proportionately. GNP fell 20.4 per cent in 1921
and rose by 3.6 in 1922 while current account payments fell by 34.0 and 9.2 per
cent. In real terms this expansionary stimulus was even greater. While real current
account payments fell by 0.9 in 1921 and 4.3 per cent in 1922, real GNP rose by
2.7 and 16.9. In addition total net long-term capital imports fell but slightly in
1921 and rose sharply in 1922 so that Canadian purchasing power in terms of foreign
currencies was reinforced strongly while current payments fell. When the monthly
estimates are examined a similar conclusion is derived. After a sharp fall in 1921
total current account debits (as well as total merchandise debits) reached a trough
in January 1922. Meanwhile relatively large long-term capital imports occurred
during the period immediately preceding and about the up-turn, even in the
pessimistic monthly estimates.
    Imports of producers' goods fell from 20.8 per cent of GNP in 1920 to 14.6 in
1921 and 12.8 in 1922 (Appendix B, Table X) while gross domestic capital formation
fell from 22.7 per cent of GNP in 1920 to 11.0 in 1921 and rose to 19.5 in 1922. In
so far as this 1922 divergence may indicate a partial switch from foreign to home
sources of supply, an expansionary stimulus may be located here. But substitution
of producers' goods is not as easy as substitution of consumers' goods so that this
factor cannot be considered important. Nor did any strong autonomous switch to the
home market occur in the consumers' good sector.

    11. See Appendix C, Table XIII.

    12. Much the same pattern holds if the trade in outstanding securities is
deleted from the long-term capital account.

    13. See Appendix A for method used in estimating monthly net long-term
capital movements and for data. Since all the errors and omissions cannot be

attributed to the capital account, these monthly estimates are too low for 1921-22.

14. On the method used to estimate monthly monetary gold movements for the pre-1926 period see Appendix A.

15. See Appendix A.

16. On the whole, adjustment to the improved situation in the balance of payments, such as it was, was obtained by fluctuations of the exchange rate. (The balance of payments is defined throughout this essay as the sum of the long-term capital and current accounts and hence need not always "be balanced" as the total of all out-payments and all in-payments must.)

17. The balancing account is the sum of the monetary gold and short-term capital flows.

18. Figures refer to net advances as of the last juridical day of the month as given in the monthly return of the chartered banks.

19. The total of current loans plus security holdings fell from a monthly average of $1722 million in 1920 to $1615 million in 1921 and $1454 million in 1922. Deflated by the wholesale price index, it rose from $1110 million in 1920 (1926 prices) to $1482 million in 1921, but then remained relatively stable at $1493 million in 1922 and $1473 million in 1923. The same behaviour is evidenced by total deposits. In current prices total deposits fell continually from 1920 to 1923 and then rose slightly in 1924. In 1926 prices, they rose from a monthly average of $1572 million in 1920 to $2078 million in 1921, but then remained relatively stable at $2178, $2135, $2146, and $2169 million in the next four years.
No annual data are published as yet on the rates charged on bank advances but they appear to have remained relatively stable for at least several decades before 1929. See S. E. Nixon, "Interest Rates in Canada: I, The Course of Interest Rates, 1929-1937," C.J.E.P.S., III, no. 3, (August, 1937), 421, 431. The rate of interest charged the commercial banks on advances under the Finance Act remained at 5 per cent until November 1, 1924, except that 3.5 per cent was charged on Imperial Treasury Bills under the terms of an Order-in-Council of October 20, 1917.

20. This conclusion is supported by the behaviour of the velocity of circulation of bank deposits whose cyclical trough came in February 1922. For the velocity figures and the method of computation, see Appendix D, Table XV. The trough of February 1923 arose from (i) a drastic fall in business and transportation caused by the "unprecedentedly cold weather" and (ii) a fuel crisis in central Canada resulting from the small coal ration doled out to Canada by the American coal trust after the prolonged coal strikes of 1922. See the Economist, March 24, 1923, 642.

21. Canada had no central bank but, as a legacy from the war, a "temporary"

arrangement whereby Dominion notes could be obtained from the Department of
Finance on deposit of approved securities. Under section 4 of the Finance Act,
1914 (Statutes of Canada, 5 Geo. V, c. 3), the Dominion Government was
authorized in time of war or panic to advance Dominion notes (legal tender money)
to the chartered banks upon the pledge of satisfactory collateral. Thus the chartered
banks, relatively few in number but with many branches, were under no central
control or pressure but still the ultimate amount of bank credit was not limited
solely by their physical resources. The expectation that the Finance Act would be
discontinued two years after the conclusion of the peace may account in part for
their desire to work off these advances.

22. Obtained from the real GNP series the marginal propensity to consume was
. 76 per cent in 1920 and . 74 per cent in 1922; in 1921 consumption fell while real
GNP rose. Real consumption was obtained by deflating the tentative D. B. S. series
(S. B. Smith, letter of 25 Nov. 1947) by the index of consumer goods prices. See
Chap. II, n. 2, on the unsatisfactory nature of this series and justification for using
it. The marginal propensity, obtained from the personal income series ("total
payments to individuals," C.Y.B., 1945, 910), fell from 1. 7 per cent in 1920 to
1. 6 in 1921; in 1922 consumption rose despite a fall in personal income.

23. Real gross domestic investment is the old D.B.S. series on "gross capital
formation" (M.R.B.S., April, 1944, 38) less changes in international claims and
in the monetary gold stock, deflated by the wholesale price index of producers'
goods.

24. Dominion Government expenditure continued to exceed its revenues after
the war until the end of the fiscal year 1924. While the Dominion Government's
net debt rose by $674 million in the fiscal year 1920 and $92 million and $81 million
in the next two fiscal years (C.Y.B., 1945, 944), the net savings of Dominion and
provincial governments together fell from $39 million in 1920 to $5 million in
1921 and then rose to $60 million in 1922 (M.R.B.S., Jan., 1944, 6). Thus no
great expansionary force is found here.

25. See chart (Fig. 2). For sources see chap. II, n. 2 and n. 22.

26. Thus since not only the percentage consumed but also the absolute level
of consumption expenditure both in real and in money terms fell in 1923 -4 despite
a rising national income, it would appear that a downward shift of the consumption
function took place at this time. Experiment with the old D.B.S. data in current
prices for lags and leads yields a lag of consumption behind GNP of approximately
seven months for the period 1919-39 as a whole. A definite downward shift of the
consumption function is still revealed at this time when allowance is made for this
lag.

27. While Dominion of Canada long-term bond prices rose by 1. 2 per cent

in 1921, preferred and common stock prices fell 10.2 and 13.6 per cent. By July 1921 Government bond prices rose 4.5 per cent from their trough in November 1920 and preferred stocks 0.5 per cent (with minor oscillations) from their trough in December. Common stocks did not rise until September 1921. Thus in both the annual and the monthly data the change in yield was more important than that in risk premium.

28. The long-term interest rate fell from 5.69 per cent in November 1920 to 5.31 in January 1921 and then remained relatively stable until October 1921.

29. Since real GNP rose by 16.9 per cent in 1922 it could be argued that the increased rate of consumption was merely the concomitant of increased incomes. But the evidence is not unequivocal. These statistics could also be construed as evidence of the application of the acceleration principle. For with an increase in consumption and a more than corresponding (induced) increase in investment, the percentage increase in GNP might well be greater than the percentage increase of consumption and consumption would be expected to decrease as a percentage of GNP. In addition the monthly index of consumers' goods production rose (after March 1921) before the rise of durable producers' goods production (after May 1921). (A lag might reasonaly be expected between the rise of sales and the rise of output because of uncertainty about the trend of demand and of the length of the gestation period involved. Without definite information as to whether this combined lag would necessarily be shorter in the consumers' goods industries, the output data may perhaps be used as a first approximation of the relative timing of recovery. More-over, to test the possibility of a stimulation of the investment industries by a prior up-turn of the consumers' goods industries, just such a physical output comparison is desirable.) Thus investment activity may have been party stimulated by the recovery of production in the consumers' goods industries. But the fact that personal expenditure on consumers' goods and services, both in money and in real terms, fell in 1923-4, while gross domestic capital formation continued to rise, suggests that this recovery of consumption was not a major determinant of investment.

Nor does the acceleration principle gain any additional credibility when domestic consumption plus exports are used as a base of acceleration since their sum fell in 1923-24 in money terms (in 1924 alone in real terms) while gross domestic capital formation and GNP rose. A slightly closer fit occurs if real exports are used as a base. They rose by 36, 15, and 0.5 per cent in the years 1922-4 while real GNP rose by 16.9, 7.0 and 0.6 per cent.

30. Depreciation allowances.(M.R.B.S., March, 1944, 15), changes in the monetary gold stock and in international claims (ibid., April, 1944, 38) have been deducted from the D.B.S. "gross capital formation" estimates (ibid.) to obtain "net domestic investment."

31. Depreciation allowances (D.B.S., National Accounts, Income and

Expenditure, 1926-1950, 26f.) have been deducted from gross home investment
(ibid., 46f.) to obtain "net domestic investment."

32. See Appendix C, Table XIV.

33. American coal producers, 98 per cent of whose exports came to Canada,
dubbed this region the "fuel acute area."

34. Construction of the new Welland Canal and schools bolstered the upswing.

35. The index of efficiency per wage earner in manufacturing industries rose
from 99.9 in 1920 to 125.6 in 1921 and 134.1 in 1922 (C.Y.B., 1938, 450).

36. See Appendix C, Table XVI, on the method used in constructing this index.
In his original trade cycle theory Hayek argued that the transition to less capitalistic methods of production induced by high interest rates precipitates depression.
In his more recent variant Hayek substitutes high and low rates of profit for low and
high interest rates. During the later stages of the upswing the price of the entre-
preneur's product rises and money wage rates lag so that product wages (money wage
rate delfated by price of product) fall. (Product wages thus obtained are significant
here rather than real wages in the customary sense (i.e., money wage rate divided
by the cost of living index), since the profit margin, not employees' welfare,
influences the investment behaviour of entrepreneurs.) This fall of product wages
raises the expected profit rate on less capital-using production methods. The
resulting switch from capital to labour involves a decline in the rate of investment
and thus precipitates a depression. Hayek calls this process the Ricardo effect. Thus
increased consumer expenditures are responsible for the down-turn via rising
consumers' goods prices and money wage lag in this new variant (via rising interest
rates in his earlier theory).
This Ricardo effect has not been revealed as a dominant determinant throughout
the period studied. It may help explain the 1921 up-turn when product wages
obtained by deflating the general money wage index by the wholesale price index
rose to 110.5 from 85.3 in 1920 (to 113 from 83.4 when the price index of domestic
goods is used as deflator, Appendix C, Table XVI) and continued to rise in 1922-3.
The up-turn of investment by mid-1921 before that of employment (after January
1922) lends support to the thesis that the adoption of more capitalistic forms of
production may have contributed to the business revival. But the Ricardo effect was
non-existent in 1926-29 when product wages rose and also in 1933-4 when product
wages fell. Perhaps the lack of applicability of this theory results partly from the
absence of a suitable measure of the variables involved. See Hayek, "The Ricardo
Effect," Economica, IX, N.S., no. 34 (May, 1942), especially 150ff., on the
statistical difficulties. One of the difficulties in Canada is that wage indexes relate
mainly to secondary industry and wholesale price indexes to all industry. For
theoretical weaknesses in this theory, however, see N. Kaldor, "Professor Hayek and
the Concertina Effect," ibid., no. 36 (November, 1942), 373-81, and G. Haberler,

<u>Prosperity and Depression</u> (Geneva, 1941), 488-91.

37. It is true that all wage cuts are double-edged. There is the danger that lowered labour receipts may mean decreased consumption and hence a deterioration of expectations for enterprises and aggravated depression. The fact that consumption rose in 1922, however, suggests that wage cuts about the time of the up-turn and the very early upswing were not serious enough to react unfavourably on consumption and hence that they may have had a favourable over-all effect upon business decisions.

38. The yearly index of hourly wages fell in the building trades from 180.9 in 1920 to 170.5 in 1921 and 162.5 in 1922, in the metal trades from 209.4 to 186.8 and 173.7, and for common factory labour from 215.3 to 190.6 and 183.0 (1913 = 100).

39. The index of rents rose sharply from 114.7 in January 1920 to 141.4 in July 1921 and kept on rising. Meanwhile the price index of building and con - struction materials fell from 229.4 in April 1920 to 178.2 in July 1921 and to 159.5 nine months later.

40. The induced domestic investment resulting from the investment financed by the long-term capital import probably more than offset the deflationary influence of any increase in merchandise imports which tend to arise and thus to effect equilibrium under these paper standard conditions.

41. Obviously psychological influences from abroad on occasion can be very important. Increasing optimism or pessimism in the United States was often trans - mitted to Canada through the medium of closely related news, radio, and financial forecasting services as well as trade papers, travelling business men, letters from American head offices to Canadian branch plants, and connected bond and stock markets. Perhaps the stock exchange may be taken as one of the best available barometers of psychological movements. The cyclical trough of common stock prices in both Canada and the United States came in the same month, August 1921. It is difficult to obtain more detailed series which are comparable. Of those offering at least some degree of comparability, pulp and paper stocks and industrial stocks were two having cyclical troughs in the same month in both countries.

But fluctuations in security prices were not very important in effecting the up-turn so that the question whether domestic or foreign factors were primarily responsible for these changes, while interesting, is not pertinent at this juncture. Moreover, the rosy expectations which may have aided the up-turn apparently were not based on the prognostications of chart readers or messages of itinerant preachers but rather upon such concrete facts as the rise of exports and tourist receipts. Thus it is to the geographical source of these pertinent factors that we must turn. The fact that they happen to be located in the international accounts by no means implies, however, that international account items are the only possible trans - mitters of cyclical impulses from one country to another. If we had found that the rosy expectations had not been based upon any such "real" phenomena then a detailed study of the mechanism of transmission of these purely psychological impulses from abroad would be warranted.

42. Using a method of averaging somewhat similar to that of Section I of this chapter, only much more refined, Burns and Mitchell (Measuring Business Cycles, 78f.) have obtained the following reference dates for the 1921 trough:

Great Britain	June 1921
France	July 1921
United States	September 1921

Since the larger part of Canada's external commercial and financial transactions probably took place with the United States (cf. A.F.W. Plumptre, Central Banking in the British Dominions, Toronto, 1947, 414), the Canadian up-turn seems to have preceded most of those abroad in so far as comparability exists in the methods used. Obviously the shortcomings of the statistical procedure preclude making any such statement as a decisive conclusion. But perhaps it may be accepted for lack of more adequate criteria. By "abroad" or "foreign" is meant the rest of the world having any major degree of importance to Canada's external monetary affairs.

43. As with Canada, no one index of the business cycle is available either for Great Britain or the United States. Hence it becomes necessary to compare available price series and especially volume series. While these series are not based on exactly the same phenomena and hence are not strictly comparable, if the majority of them exhibit the same tendencies, a tentative conclusion can be drawn.
    An attempt has been made to obtain series as comparable as possible for Canada, Britain, and the United States. The percentage changes in 1921-2 are given in Appendix C, Table XII. In only five of the twelve major series was the increase in Canada less than that in Britain and/or the United States. None of these five is an over-all volume aggregate. Hence it would appear that Canada's upswing in 1922 proceeded at a faster rate than those abroad. (The greater increase in Canadian business indicators, 1921-2, is no doubt attributable partly to the earlier Canadian up-turn. But since most of the series reveal much sharper gains in Canada, it does not appear logical to attribute this divergence in intensity merely to the slight difference in the timing of the troughs.)

44. Source: D.B.S., Monthly Report of the Trade of Canada. The relation-ship between the cyclical troughs in these areas and the troughs of Canada's trade with them may be of some interest. Canada's up-turn preceded and her initial upswing was more intense than the American; the trough of American imports came (January 1922) before that of exports to America. The British up-turn preceded the Canadian and the trough of British imports came (June 1921) after that of exports to Britain. While France's up-turn coincided with Canada's, the early French upswing was stronger; and exports to France rose sevenfold within a year of their trough

(January 1922) while imports from France only doubled within a year of their trough (June 1922). The cyclical troughs of all these flows are only first approximations since the data are not adjusted for seasonality.

45. It might seem that the Canadian export figures do not offer much of a criterion of the impact of cyclical swings abroad upon the Canadian economy -- especially in reference to a single month chosen as the trough -- unless allowance is made for possible lags. But these exports do not appear to have lagged behind the national income of these respective areas since no significant counter-clockwise pattern occurs in the scatter diagrams with exports on the axis of ordinates.

46. See Appendix C, Table XIII.

47. Total exports of wood products rose in July 1921; those to the United States rose in June. From June to December manufactured wood exports to Britain, the United States, and Other Countries rose 92, 79, and 42.5 per cent; paper exports, 21, 29, and 92 per cent.

48. These percentages refer to the fiscal year ending March 31, 1922. C.Y.B., 1924, 474-77.

49. The increase in aluminum exports went mainly to Other Countries, chiefly Australia and India, although those to the United States also rose. By December lead exports to Britain rose by $62 thousand over May's level, those to Other Countries (chiefly Japan) rose by $88 thousand, and those to the United States fell sharply. Britain took most of the increased exports of electrical apparatus; the increases to the United States and Other Countries were relatively small.

50. No data on the source of tourist receipts are available before 1926 but in that year credits from American tourists accounted for 94 per cent of total tourist credits (D.B.S., The Canadian Balance of International Payments: A Study of Methods and Results, Ottawa, 1939, 67, 69).

51. Long-term capital invested in Canada by Britain fell $83.8 million in 1921 and $29.7 million in 1922, that by Other Countries fell $12.4 and $2.0 million, that by the United States rose $132 and $333 million. The cyclical trough of new Canadian long-term capital imports from the United States came in May 1921, two months before Canada's trade cycle trough. While the net long-term capital import from all sources from February to July totalled $62.8 million, new capital imports from the United States were $50.3 million (see Appendix A, Table XIII).

Chapter Three

1. Most of the first two subsections is a summary of my "External Determinants of the Canadian Upswing,1921-9," C.J.E.P.S., XVII, no. 1(February 1951), 50-64.

2. So slow was the first half of the Canadian upswing on the whole that it amounted to a relapse in some quarters. While the number of commercial failures in Canada fell from a peak of 3,630 in 1922 to 3,197 in 1923 and 2,445 in 1924, the absolute number was still very high compared with 751 for 1919 and 2,100 for 1928. (C.Y.B., 1932, 826.)

3. The years 1921-4 and 1924-9 were used originally as the two halves of the upswing but the same pattern holds if 1925 is used as the dividing year.

4. Exports led GNP in current prices by approximately eight months. (This is only an approximation since annual data were used without allowance for seasonal movements.)

5. Even those occasionally strong inflows which may have bolstered the upswing in some years were probably not totally independent of commodity exports or the outlook for exports.

6. If one postulated a lag of some three years, the monetary gold and short-term capital flows might appear to have had a somewhat more active role.

7. Both in money and in real terms the percentage consumed fell more sharply than would be expected of an upward movement along a stable consumption function.

The multiplier and relation are marginal principles relating to small oscillations and usually postulating a marginal propensity to consume constant with the level of national income and over the time period covered. Annual figures may well be too large for the close testing of such relationships since the oscillations for certain combinations of the multiplier and relation may be such as to destroy the validity of the test. Hence I am definitely not trying to test multiplier and acceleration theory, merely trying rather to indicate the fundamental reason for the fall in consumption despite increased national income and investment.

8. See Fig. 2. The function relating income payments to individuals to GNP remained stable in 1922-4.

Throughout the period 1919-39 as a whole, consumption in current prices seems to have lagged behind GNP by approximately seven months in the old D.B.S. data and approximately five months in the revised (1948) D.B.S. data for the period beginning in 1926. This is an approximate finding partly because only annual data were available and hence monthly averages were computed by dividing the annual totals by twelve. It is interesting to note that a lead rather than a lag appears for the years 1921-3 not only when the data are plotted with a seven-month lag but

also in the original data. In so far as evidence of a lead or lag with reference to
GNP could be taken to represent to some extent at least relative degrees of active-
ness in the determination of GNP, this evidence corroborates the conclusion that
fluctuations in consumption were important in determining the general level of
activity in the first part of the upswing.

9. Investment associated with the application of innovations seems to have been
largely autonomous and not tied directly to some prior rise of exports or consumption.
See my "Internal Determinants of the Canadian Upswing," C.J.E.P.S., XVI, no. 2
(May 1950), 196ff., on how the development of Canada's leading manufacturing
industry, newsprint, and also of the hydro-electric power industry appears to fit
Schumpeter's description of the Kondratieff cycle and to be consistent with the
dates given for his "Neomercantilist Kondratieff" in the United States.

10. On the generally unsatisfactory nature of the rate of change of consumption
expenditure as the sole explanation of most investment sub-divisions, even when
allowance is made for the existence of unused capacity at low levels of output,
see ibid., 187-96. Nor is the result significantly improved if allowance is made for
a possible lag of investment or for the role of commodity exports in inducing
domestic investment. This test is not completely satisfactory since some portions
of induced investment may require planning of vastly different periods of time. Thus
the induced investment of any particular "week" of calendar time may be related
functionally to a great many different previous "weeks." And, of course, multiplier
and acceleration theory is quite consistent with a situation where induced private
investment is small.

11. Residential contracts and "engineering and industrial contracts" fell,
1923-4; "business" contracts, 1920-5.

12. O. J. Firestone, Residential Real Estate in Canada (Toronto, 1951), 57.

13. Most of this section is a summary of my "Mechanism of Adjustment in
Canada's Balance of Payments, 1921-9," C.J.E.P.S., XVIII, no. 3 (August 1952),
303-21.

14. The long-term capital account might well be dubbed the "minor independent variable" since it was not the major force determining the exchange rate but
still was not directly related to the fluctuations of other international account items.

15. See Appendix A.

16. Familiarity with American technology, the adoption of American-designed
equipment, and the large sectors of Canadian industry owned by Americans account
for the demand for American-type producers' goods.

17. No doubt many capital imports induced merchandise imports but this was not the dominant factor determining the level of imports.

18. Direct adjustment was not the major means of adjustment in either part of the upswing.

19. Balancing movements occurred in outstanding security transactions and perhaps also in the transfer of branch plant funds as well as in the regular short-term capital category.

20. The banks paid off these advances partly because they knew, once Canada went on a de facto gold standard in mid-1923, that they could get back any imported gold they paid in to the Department of Finance so that there was no incentive to hold sterile gold or to hold large balances abroad unless the earnings on those assets were higher than the rate paid on Finance Act advances or unless there was a fairly good prospect of an appreciation of the Canadian dollar.

21. The industries rapidly expanding at this time, pulp and paper and non-ferrous metals, customarily resorted to the security and stock markets for most of their funds.

22. A change in income distribution contributed particularly in 1922 when the fall of the function relating income payments to individuals to GNP effected a similar shift in the function relating imports to GNP. Commodity imports remained a fairly close function of income payments to individuals in 1920-5.
    The expected lag of imports behind exports (cf. J. F. Parkinson, "Canada's International Accounts and the Foreign Exchanges," Canadian Investment and Foreign Exchange Problems, Toronto, 1940, chap. II, 18) can hardly be considered a sufficient explanation of the failure of imports to rise because of their stability for such a prolonged period.

23. As foreign interest in Canada's slow upswing diminished, interest of Canadians in foreign upswings quickened, and increased domestic savings out of rising national income together with relatively low investment demand provided funds for the redemption of securities and rendered imports of foreign savings less necessary.

24. Still the expansion was facilitated to a considerable extent by a rise in velocity as comparison with United States figures shows. See D. C. MacGregor, "The Problem of Price Level in Canada," C.J.E.P.S., XIII, no. 2 (May 1947), 190 and also 187f.

25. The "marginal efficiency of capital" could fall because of a deterioration of business expectations or increase in costs as well as decreased physical returns and decreased marginal revenue.

26. In his cursory treatment of "The Canadian Balance of Payments," chap. XII of Cyclical Movements in the Balance of Payments (Cambridge, 1951), Mr. T. C. Chang appears to reason thus: Expansion in the United States was more violent than in Canada in 1928 and the first half of 1929 and hence Canadians bought large quantities of American securities (209ff.). In fact, the Canadian expansion was more violent in 1928 than the American. American GNP and national income rose by 2.1 and 2.0 per cent (Kuznets data); in Canada they rose by 8.1 and 9.2 per cent. Moreover net purchases of foreign securities fell sharply in 1928 according to the revised D.B.S. estimates.

Incidentally Chang's statement that his 1926-38 balance of payments data came from Public Expenditure and Capital Formation is suspect. First, no such volume exists to my knowledge; he evidently was referring to Public Investment and Capital Formation since all his other references to the former "source" are appropriate for this publication. Secondly, his capital and monetary gold items cannot have come even from this volume since no such data appear in it.

Basing all correlations upon the 1926-38 period taken as a whole, Chang concludes that the typical cyclical pattern for Canada's current account balance is a surplus in prosperity and deficit during slump (203f.) -- a most extraordinary conclusion since Canada's current account balance became progressively less active or more passive in the boom period 1926-9 and the reverse during the downswing 1930-3, the temporary worsening in 1930 being caused mainly by a rise in dividend and interest payments. Chang's peculiar conclusion is thus based mainly on the short cycle 1933-8 which saw no real boom. Even here, however, the fall in the current account balance in 1937 was caused chiefly by the sharp increase of merchandise imports with the first blush of boom conditions. The increasing surplus of the current account balance, 1933-6, reminds one of the "period of the advance," 1921-5, when no real boom had as yet developed. Having derived a "pattern" which fits less than half of the years he has dealt with, a peculiar period in itself, Chang takes pains to explain the 1927-8 "exceptions" to his generalizations by the youth of Canadian manufacturing industry in those days, indicated by our dependence upon American capital goods for our development boom. A brief glance at Canada's post-war international accounts shows that our manufacturing industry is still "young" since we are still dependent upon the United States for many of our capital goods. The 1933-8 cycle was the unusual one since it lacked any really strong investment boom.

Unfortunately, many of Chang's other conclusions are also suspect because they are similarily based upon correlations struck for the 1926-38 period as a whole. If one insists upon deriving a single generalization by correlation analysis to fit a lengthy period, surely it would be preferable to feed a single complete cycle (e.g., 1921-33) or integral multiples thereof into the calculator -- especially if one is looking for cyclical behaviour.

27. For reasons why the net movement was not in a balancing direction in 1927 and 1928 see chap. VII.

Chapter Four

1. Only four changes have been made in the set used for ascertaining the 1921 cyclical trough. First, one production index, sheep slaughterings, revealed no definite cyclical peak. Rather than introduce too great a degree of judgment, this series has been deleted. Secondly, the D.B.S. monthly series on retail sales which is available from January 1929 has been used. Thirdly, the seasonally adjusted index of "Dominion notes in the hands of the public" has been used to replace the unadjusted series on the simple total of the Dominion note issue. The former appears to be a more relevant concept as far as the effective volume of money in circulation is concerned and, in addition, has the advantage of being seasonally adjusted. Lastly, seasonally adjusted indexes on demand deposits and on current loans have been used in place of the unadjusted raw data used formerly. See Table II.

2. Perhaps the down-turn was concealed to some extent by the seasonality of the current data.

3. Another explanation of the down-turn sometimes offered turns on the fact that the current account balance fell continuously after 1925. Thus the seeds of destruction were sown just as Canada was casting off the lethargy of the early 20's. A sad fate indeed that, once out of the depression, a rise of income must necessarily imply a rise of imports and hence certain disaster! One might even wonder whether it was worth while leaving the state of depression if such a "wrong twist" must begin almost from the very moment of emergence. This statement is as meaningless as the observation that human death is governed by conception. One error of this explanation lies in disregarding the behaviour of total real investment in all directions.

4. D.B.S., National Accounts, Income and Expenditure, 1926-1950 (Ottawa, 1952), 28.

5. The deflationary effect of the rising current account purchases, largely the concomitant of Canadian prosperity, was of minor significance. With merchandise exports relatively stable in their usual seasonal pattern until April 1929, rising merchandise imports could only exert deflationary pressure in so far as they were not offset by enlarged purchasing power from such sources as long-term capital imports. While the rise in long-term capital imports excluding outstanding security trans-actions more than offset the rise in current account purchases in 1929 as a whole, the monthly estimates reveal a possible deflationary pressure since long-term capital imports from January to May 1929 did not make up for the increased commodity imports then.

No second deflationary influence resulted from Canadians switching their demands from home to foreign goods according to comparison of the percentage of GNP devoted to imports of consumers' goods and also of producers' goods (Appendix B, Table X) with their domestic equivalents.

6. Since the cyclical peak in commercial gold exports came in January 1928

their decline might appear, at first sight, to have contributed to the Canadian down-turn. But this is just the behaviour one would expect from a commodity produced under conditions of fixed demand price. With boom conditions, greater scarcity of factors would tend to increase the costs of production in gold mining and perhaps check production. This sequence might be expected in Canada since, generally speaking, alternative employment would be available under boom conditions for many of the factors employed in gold mining. Moreover, since gold mining was not the dominant industry, a down-turn in it would not necessitate a down-turn for Canadian business in general. Rather it would be the result of a boom in most of the remaining industries. Hence the fall in commercial gold exports was not a dominant depressing factor; rather it was the concomitant of the boom.

7. Over one hundred ships were docked in Montreal, many with crews paid off. Financial Post, May 16, 1929, p. 7.

8. The new tariff passed the House of Representatives about the end of May. It had been threatening Canada ever since Hoover's election in November 1928.

9. "In pursuing this policy, however, the wheat pool appeared to be doing no more than carrying on careful merchandising. The pools' unrivalled system of recording and estimating Canadian crop conditions enabled them to forecast the small 1929 crop." .W. A. Mackintosh, Economic Problems of the Prairie Provinces (Toronto, 1935), 53.

10. At one time the July option got so far out of line that, had there been time to complete the transaction, it would have paid to turn around a cargo of wheat at Liverpool and deliver it at Port Arthur (Financial Post, July 11, 1929, 1). So large was the spread between Winnipeg and Chicago prices that many American farmers shipped their grain over the border to Canadian elevators (Economist, Oct. 26, 1929, 769).

11. Financial Post, July 25, 1929, 1.

12. Unexpected reserves in Russia and Argentina supplied the demand while Canadians were still holding their wheat in December. Both the United States and Argentina attempted to hold back their wheat but the latter's lack of storage space forced her to market the crop.
On some of the long-run underlying maladjustments see W. A. Mackintosh, The Economic Background of Dominion-Provincial Relations (Ottawa, 1939), 55ff.

13. Economist, October 26, 1929, 770.

14. See Appendix C, Table XIII.

15. The fall in automobile production for the domestic market was much

greater than in that for the export market.

16. When the net purchases of outstanding securities are excluded, the gross capital outflow fell from $220 million in 1928 to $161 million in 1929, and the net inflow rose from $22 to $188 million.

17. Monetary gold exports of $54.1 million and short-term capital imports of $16.2 million in the first six months of 1929 helped stop the gap in Canada's balance of payments. These movements do not appear abnormally large at first sight and might even be considered small for a regular seasonal flow. But they do not tell the whole story. The Canadian dollar was never within the gold points on the average during any month of 1929. Rather it continued to depreciate fairly regularly after December 1928. Since these movements were not large in relation to usual seasonal flows, however, no great net transfer of purchasing power took place and the minor depressing effect of the rising merchandise imports was, to that extent, lessened.

18. Actually the same value for the index of aggregate issues of Dominion notes prevailed in November 1928 but the latest peak perhaps may be taken in such instances.

19. While total security holdings (and the seasonally-adjusted index of these holdings) reached a peak in February 1928, their subsequent decline reflected mainly the profitableness of shifting to the loan-shoulder during prosperity. Moreover, the peak of security holdings plus all loans in Canada came in October 1929.

20. The international reserves lost were mainly secondary reserves. Because of the ease with which Dominion notes could be secured under the Finance Act, it is hardly surprising that total cash reserves in Canada rose along with the rise in total public liabilities in 1929 so that the cash reserve ratio remained relatively stable. See my "Mechanism of Adjustment in Canada's Balance of Payments, 1921-9," C.J.E.P.S., XVIII, no. 3 (August 1952), 308.

21. July was the only month in 1929 when the monthly average of these total daily advances was less than in the corresponding month of 1928. Report of the Royal Commission on Banking and Currency in Canada (Ottawa, 1933), 43.

22. While most bank rates were relatively steady, those on brokers loans were raised to reduce stock speculation.

23. Ibid., 41.

24. In terms of current prices, the marginal propensity to consume was .66 in 1927, .60 in 1928, and 3.26 in 1929.

25. The shift occurs in the revised 1952 D.B.S. estimates also. It was a shift of the function relating consumption to personal disposable income that was responsible for the corresponding shift of the function relating consumption to GNP. It is interesting to note that when consumption is lagged three months behind personal disposable income in the revised 1952 estimates no strong shift in the consumption function appears during the 1926-30 period.

26. Investment in business inventories, in "grain in commercial channels and farm inventories" (Dominion-Provincial Conference on Reconstruction, Public Investment and Capital Formation: A Study of Public and Private Investment Out-lay, Canada, 1926-1941, Ottawa, 1945, 30f.), and new investment in durable physical assets for agriculture, pulp and paper, and printing and publishing (Department of Trade and Commerce, Private and Public Investment in Canada, 1926-1951, Ottawa, 1951, 153 and 160f.) all fell from their 1928 peaks. At least part of this investment was of the induced variety.

27. The fact that the production of consumers' goods fell off after April and that of durable producers' goods after January 1929, as one might expect from the theory of the "Relation," does not substantiate this theory, if the sharp rise of consumption after May is considered significant. (In so far as retail sales may be taken as a criterion of consumption demand, the expectation of a down-turn of this series before that of the output of consumers' goods was not fulfilled.) Without monthly data for 1927-8, it is impossible to tell if a significant fall in the rate of increase of retail sales occurred before January 1929.

28. Total personal savings fell from a peak of $365 million in 1928 to $196 million in 1929 (National Accounts, Income and Expenditure, 1926-1950, 30), mainly because of a $129 million disinvestment of farm inventories. This disinvestment explains in part the upward shift in 1929 of the functions relating consumption to personal disposable income and to GNP. It is difficult to determine when farm inventories are regarded as income by farmers -- when they are accumulated or when they are liquidated. If farmers treat inventories as income only when they realize cash, a fall of investment is accompanied by an increase of consumption. This peculiarity seems to account for some of the aberrations in the function relating consumption to GNP.
   The seasonally adjusted index of notice deposits fell from a peak of 130.1 in December 1928 to 122 the following May (1922-5 = 100). Corporation profits before taxes were at a peak of $530 million in 1928-9 (ibid., 52).

29. The down-turn cannot be attributed to government oversaving. Dominion Government revenue continued to exceed expenditure and its net debt was scaled down by $51 million in 1928 and $71 million in 1929 (C.Y.B., 1945, 944). The surplus of all governments combined fell from $84 million in 1928 to $9 million in 1929, and deficits of $222 million and $311 million occurred in 1930 and 1931. (National Accounts, Income and Expenditure, 1926-1950, 36).

30. Although total new bond issues rose from $424 million in 1928 to $628 million in 1929, those for "industrial and miscellaneous" borrowers fell from $213 million to $132 million (Report of the Royal Commission on Banking and Currency in Canada, 107).   But this might well be the result of the switch to stock financing. Secondly, although the peak of new bond issues came in June 1929 most of the peak borrowers resorted to foreign capital markets. Of the cyclical peak of $136 million in June, 82 per cent consisted of new placements in the United States and $105 million represented new corporate long-term bonds placed there. Of the new bond issues in the first six months of 1929, roughly 64 per cent was placed in the United States compared with 38 in the same period of 1928. (Data on new Canadian bond placements in the United States, compiled from the Commercial and Financial Chronicle, have not been corrected for exchange rate fluctuations.) But since the long-term interest rate rose only 0.27 percentage points in 1928-9 in the United States compared with 0.36 in Canada, some such switching to the American capital market would be expected.

31. The change of the long-term rate of interest in 1919-20 was 0.51 percentage points.

32. No strong price inflation took place partly because of the availability of merchandise imports. Cf. R. B. Bryce, "Some Aspects of Canadian Economic Relations with the United States," Foreign Economic Policy for the United States, ed. S. E. Harris (Cambridge, Mass., 1948), 142.
It is true that with increased efficiency, prices might fall in a period of inflation and that the Canadian price rise was actually greater than that in Britain or the United States in both the annual and the monthly indexes. The sharpest price rise took place in July in Canada (4.1 per cent), Britain (1.3), and the United States (1.7). Only Canadian prices continued to rise in August. But the sharp rise of Canadian prices reflected mainly the continued drought on the Prairies; the price rise of non-vegetables was fractional. Since these price rises were restricted to certain markets and came well after the down-turn of business, it does not seem plausible to cite them as evidence of widespread inflation. The sharp increases of consumers' goods and producers' goods prices are also doubtful evidence of inflation since they occurred several months after the down-turn of general business.

33. The general weighted average of wage rates rose from an index of 190.4 in 1927 to 192.2 in 1928, 196.0 in 1929 and 197.1 in 1930 as against 173.4 to 207.7 in 1919 and 1920.

34. Appendix C, Table XVI.

35. The building trades wage rate index was 179.3, 185.6, 197.5 and a peak of 203.2 in the four years 1927-30. The index of wage rates of common factory labour rose from 187.1 to 187.8 and 188.2 in the years 1928-30, of miscellaneous factory trades from 200.9 to 202.1 and 202.3, of metal trades from 180.1 to 184.6

and 186.6.

36. Nor was the down-turn caused by a "rationalization process," i.e., the introduction of labour-saving machines on a large scale. The more rapid rise in manufacturing production (23 per cent in 1926-9) than in employment (20 per cent) may have been caused partly by increased efficiency (3 per cent) resulting in part from the introduction of labour-saving machines. But because of the even more rapid rise (25 per cent) in the total manufacturing wage bill, purchasing power per unit of output did not decline. There is no evidence here of oversaving or the sacrificing of wages for abnormal profits.

37. If continued production were taken as evidence of rising demand and hence opportunities for investment, no lack of investment outlets would appear in any of the innovating industries except automobiles. Because production continues on a high level, however, is no guarantee that it would be advisable to expand plant. Such an extension would depend upon market forecasts and profit positions of the corporations or individuals concerned.

38. E. A. Forsey, "The Pulp and Paper Industry," C.J.E.P.S., I, no. 3 (August 1935), 503.

39. Daily tonnage capacity rose from 5.8 thousand tons in 1924 to 6.4, 8.0, 9.9, 10.9 and 11.8 in the following years (ibid., 502).

40. The New York price fell from $71.80 in 1927 to $69 in the first half of 1928, $66 in the second half, and $62 at the beginning of 1929. The f.o.b. mill price fell from $65 to $64, $61, and $55.20 in the same period (see J. A. Guthrie, The Newsprint Paper Industry, Cambridge, Mass., 1941, 248).

41. Further evidence that these circumstances gave rise to pessimism in the pulp and paper industry is afforded by its employment index which reached a definite peak in August 1928 and by its common stock price index which fell sharply after April 1928 while most other stock and employment indexes continued to rise to peaks in 1929. Even by January 1929 low prices had closed a number of newsprint mills (Financial Post, February 1, 1929, 7). One month later it seemed certain that the capital expenditures of the newsprint industry would be largely curtailed and perhaps eliminated entirely by the end of the year (ibid., March 1, 1929, 7). New investment in durable physical assets in the "Pulp and paper and their products industries" fell from a peak of $49 million in 1928 to $25.6 million in 1929; in "Wood and its products industries" from a peak of $27.7 to $11.1 and $13.1 million in the years 1927-9 (Private and Public Investment in Canada, 1926-1951, 160).

42. A. F. Burns and W. C. Mitchell have derived the following cyclical peaks (Measuring Business Cycles, New York, 1946, 78 f.):

Germany	April 1929
United States	June 1929
Great Britain	July 1929
France	March 1930

43. All but four of the series reveal a sharper rate of decline in the United States than in Canada but the decrements in the American series were only slightly sharper than those in the Canadian. Thus the early American decline was only slightly sharper than the Canadian. On the other hand, the decline in Britain seems to have been much more gradual. Just two series reveal sharper declines in Britain than in Canada, "wholesale prices" and "employment." See Appendix C, Table XII.

44. The Canadian business down-turn preceded the American, British, and French down-turns and her imports from the United States, the United Kingdom and France reached peaks (in May 1929, October 1928, and October 1928) before those of the respective export flows to these areas. (The buyers' strike in wheat largely accounts for the peak of Canadian exports to Britain coming before that of exports to the United States although the British business cycle peak followed the American.) Conversely, Germany's down-turn preceded the Canadian and the peak of exports to Germany came before that of imports from Germany (May 1929).

45. Five separate categories of exports to Other Countries and six to Britain fell before Canada's cyclical peak. Only two categories of exports to the United States fell before Canada's cyclical down-turn. Appendix C, Table XIII.

Chapter Five

1. The same conclusion is derived if allowance is made for the fact that the British business cycle trough came in 1932.

2. Of the twelve major series examined, only two, industrial production and construction, indicated a greater decline in Canada than in the United States. But the difference in the percentage falls of most of the series was not great. See Appendix C, Table XII.

3. D.B.S., National Accounts, Income and Expenditure, 1926-1950 (Ottawa, 1952), 26ff., 46.

4. Data from ibid., 28.

5. These export figures are adjusted for balance of payments purposes only and hence differ slightly from those used in previous paragraphs which are also adjusted for national account purposes.

6. Neither the increased tariffs nor Empire preference influenced the current account much. See D. R. Annett, British Preference in Canadian Commercial Policy (Toronto, 1948), 79ff., 136f.

7. Cf. now E. Marcus, "The Cyclical Adjustment Pattern of an 'Open Economy': Canada, 1927-1939," Economic Journal, LXII, no. 246 (June 1952), 307.

8. The sharp depreciation of the Canadian dollar was the result of the depreciation of the pound sterling after September 21. On the background and multifarious forces connected with Britain's abandonment of gold, see my "British Overvaluations and Devaluations," International Journal, V, no. 1 (Winter 1949-50), 48-60, and also "Background of the British Devaluation," R.M.C. Review, XXXI (1950), 125-30 (reprinted in The Queen's Commerceman, V, no. 1, Winter 1950, 23ff., 44ff.).

9. Thus in 1932 exports to Britain rose and those to America fell although the Canadian dollar had depreciated relative to the American dollar and appreciated relative to the pound.

10. American, British, and Other Countries' long-term investment in Canada fell by $183, $92 and $7 million in the years 1931-3.

11. The monetary gold and short-term capital flows do not seem to have been important in determining the downswing pattern. If they had been, vigorous prosperity would have prevailed in 1930, intense depression in 1931, and less intense depression in 1932-3.

12. Data from D.B.S., The Canadian Balance of International Payments, Preliminary Statement, 1946 (Ottawa, 1947), 25ff.

13. The prohibitive tariffs of $1.62, $1.07, and $0.85 per bushel imposed on wheat by Germany, Italy, and France in 1930 were later supplemented with quantitative restrictions which almost completely closed these important markets. Report of the Royal Commission on Dominion-Provincial Relations, Book I (Ottawa, 1940), 145.

14. See my "External Determinants of the Canadian Upswing, 1921-9," C.J.E.P.S., XVII, no. 1, (February 1951), 57.

15. Moreover, the favourable turn of the British terms of trade, and the Ottawa Agreement resulting from the British Empire Economic Conference in July and August 1932, may have tended to encourage increased exports to Britain. It must also be noted that real exports to Britain in 1929 were abnormally low. Partly because of the selling restraint policy of the Canadian Wheat Pools, Canada's share of the British wheat market fell from 39.6 to 24.3 per cent, 1928-9, while

Argentina's share rose from 23.6 to 40.6 (Paul de Hevesy, World Wheat Planning and Economic Planning in General, London, 1940, 752).

    16. The current account was the major determinant of the exchange-rate in 1933.

    17. The sharp rise in the Canadian dollar by 0.5 cents in March 1930, when the monthly long-term capital account balance reached its yearly peak, was primarily responsible for the rise in the average yearly value of the Canadian dollar and for the divergence between the yearly and monthly correlations.

    18. Any influence the current account may have had on bank rates (through gold exports) does not appear to have been transmitted to the long-term capital market since no close correlation between bank rates and the long-term bond prices is evidenced in 1930-2. Moreover any influence of the exchange rate on long-term capital flows cannot be attributed to any great extent to the current account since the latter was not the major influence on the exchange rate throughout the downswing as a whole.

    19. The same conclusion holds if the trade in outstanding securities is excluded from the long-term capital account.

    20. Canada was able to borrow abroad much longer than Australia and Argentina after the onset of the depression because of her smaller borrowings in the previous years and because of her "sound money" policy. See F. A. Knox, Dominion Monetary Policy, 1929-1934 (Ottawa: Royal Commission on Dominion-Provincial Relations, 1939), 18.

    21. Because of the lack of any close correspondence between the net long-term capital import and merchandise imports, direct adjustment cannot have been a major means of adjustment.

    22. The specie premium rose relatively to the general price level not only in 1931 and 1932 but also in 1930.

    23. Net sales of outstanding securities occurred in each of the years so that again no evidence of a finely geared short-run equilibrating mechanism appears in this item. Net sales of $56 million occurred in 1930 compared with net purchases of $2 million in 1929 although the Canadian dollar rose in 1930. In 1931, when the exchange rate fell and foreigners might therefore be expected to buy Canadian securities, net sales dropped from $56 to $45 million as confidence in Canada waned. They rose to $85 million in 1932, however, when the Canadian dollar depreciated further. Still, net sales occurred in 1931-2 when such credits were needed to fill the gap in Canada's balance of payments. Branch plant funds may also have moved in an equilibrating fashion. See D. B. S., The Canadian Balance of International Payments: A Study of Methods and Results (Ottawa, 1939), 139f., 145, 151.

24. Both internal and outside reserves and the respective reserve ratios rose slightly during 1930. The cash reserve ratio was 7.7 per cent at the end of December 1930 compared with 7.3 a year earlier; the secondary reserve ratio rose from 7.6 to 8.6 per cent in the same period (see my "Mechanism of Adjustment in Canada's Balance of Payments, 1921-9," C.J.E.P.S., XVIII, no. 3, August 1952, 308).

While loan rates in general of one of the major banking systems fell .05 percentage points in 1930 this reduction might well reflect mainly a variation in call loan rates.

25. The reserve ratio fell from 9.1 per cent in 1930 to 8.5 per cent in 1931, if the gold holdings in the Central Gold Reserves are included. Still, the secondary reserve ratio rose slightly (Appendix C, Table XVII).

26. Since no net inflow of monetary gold materialized in the last quarter of 1931 (unlike the previous years) to bolster reserves, the banks again borrowed size-able amounts under the Finance Act for the first time since July 1930. The fall in gold held by the Department of Finance from a seasonally adjusted index of 99.2 in September 1930 to 65.4 one year later probably helped induce the Department to make a second break with gold standard conventions on October 19, 1931, by an Order-in-Council prohibiting gold exports without licence. On October 26 the plight of the banks was eased somewhat by reducing the rates charged on Finance Act advances from 4 1/2 to 3 per cent.

27. Both the secondary reserves and the secondary reserve ratio fell relatively sharply in 1932 (Appendix C, Table XVII).

28. A contractive policy seems to have been initiated by the Bank of Montreal late in 1929. In December 1929 Finance Act advances fell to $82 million from the $111 million level in November. Over 85 per cent of the advances paid off then were by this banking system. Moreover, of the $40 million decline in current loans in Canada in this month for all the chartered banks, $12 million consisted of the loans of the Bank of Montreal. Perhaps this initial thrust caused a drain on other banks at the clearing house centres and encouraged or forced them to contract credit also. Unfortunately no definite veridct can be passed as to culpability because of insufficient evidence. Moreover, the fact that another member of the big four in banking, the Canadian Bank of Commerce, had cut other loans and discounts in Canada by $21 million in the previous month means that the contractive operation of the banking mechanism was not set off by the Bank of Montreal alone. Actually other loans in Canada made by the Bank of Montreal fell 27 per cent from October 1929 to December 1930 while those of the Canadian Bank of Commerce fell 30 per cent and those of all banks by 22 per cent. As the depression deepened and collateral values fell the banks promoted "clean-up-men" as managers to liquidate as many loans as possible.

29. Still the banks definitely did curtail credit throughout the down-swing; for example, some of the banking systems stopped completely any loans to "renters" (Western tenant-farmers) whom they had lent to freely during the latter part of the upswing. Loans rates in general of one of the major banking systems fell .22 percentage points in 1931 but rose by .14 percentage points in 1932.

30. The relative rise of the general wholesale price index above the other two (1929 = 100) evidences the fall of import prices relatively to domestic goods prices:

	1930	1931	1932
Export prices	83.9	65.6	59.5
Import prices	88.9	76.9	74.8
General wholesale prices	90.6	75.4	69.8

31. If domestic prices had followed general wholesale prices, equilibrium tendencies would have resulted as relatively high import prices would have dis- couraged importing. The depressing effect on domestic prices of the primary and secondary (multiplier-accelerator) purchasing power reductions as well as the contraction of means of payment and the bullish effect on import prices of the fall in the Canadian dollar were forces tending to produce such a relative rise of import prices over domestic prices.

32. Along with the fall in demand for luxury imports and the relative stability of demand for exports, most of which were processed into consumers' goods.

33. The current account balance was slightly more passive in 1930 mainly because of a rise in interest and dividend payments.

34. Although the increased government borrowing or the increase in interest and dividend payments in 1930 cannot be attributed readily to current cyclical conditions.

Chapter Six

1. Only two minor changes have been made in the series used for ascert- aining the 1929 down-turn. First, the series on sheep slaughterings yielded a fairly definite turning-point here, as it did not in 1929, and hence has been reinstated. Secondly, seasonally adjusted indexes are available for this period for six of the employment series. As a result of these changes, only 8 of the 71 series in Table IV are neither a seasonally adjusted nor a volume index.

2. The yearly total of interest and dividend receipts also rose in 1933 but only very slightly. The reduction in total imports did not afford an expansionary

stimulus. It seemed to be merely the concomitant of reduced incomes and long-term capital imports. Nor does any switch in demand from foreign to home goods appear when the percentages of GNP devoted to imports of consumers' goods and also of producers' goods (Appendix B, Table X) are compared with their domestic equivalents. It is difficult to attribute the Canadian up-turn to the gradual improvement of the current account balance after its trough in March 1930 since Canada's cyclical up-turn did not occur until exactly three years after the up-turn of the monthly current account balance.

3.   To some extent this increase in commercial gold exports can be attributed to the depreciation of the Canadian dollar and the rise of the world price of gold.

4.   The December 1932 trough of merchandise exports is based upon the deseasonalized monthly merchandise exports adjusted for balance of payments purposes.

5.   Although freight receipts in March 1932 were $0.1 million lower than in February 1933, no significant rise occurred between these dates.

6.   Appendix C, Table XIII.

7.   The net balance of the short-term capital and monetary gold accounts was a credit of $1.7 million compared with $44.7 million for the same period a year previous.

8.   In the period from November 1932 to March 1933 the monthly current account balance fluctuated inversely with the price of the New York dollar in Canada in all but one of the monthly fluctuations.

9.   On May 1, 1933, in a revolutionary step, the rate allowed on savings deposits was reduced from 3 to 2 1/2 per cent. Thereafter rate reductions were more frequent. Nixon attributes the lowering of the rate on bank loans and advances mainly to " the substantial decline in demand for bank accommodation" (S.E. Nixon, "Interest Rates in Canada: I, The Course of Interest Rates, 1929-1937," C.J.E.P.S., III, no. 3, August 1937, 431.) Loan rates in general of one of the major banking systems fell .17 percentage points in 1933 but this might have occurred mainly after April or might also reflect mainly the variation in call loan rates.

        Perhaps borrowing was also encouraged by altering the canons of liquidity necessary for collateral. Without information as to such alterations, no conclusion can as yet be drawn.

10.   The rate on Finance Act advances remained at 3 1/2 per cent until May 1933 with the exception of advances secured by 4 per cent Treasury Bills dated October 15, 1932, or by 4 per cent two-year notes dated November 1, 1932.

11.   The British Empire Economic Conference held in Ottawa in July and
August 1932 condemned deliberate currency depreciation and advocated "easy money"
policies (primarily to raise prices), safeguarded by appropriate steps to" restrain and
circumscribe the scope of violent speculative movements in commodities or securities."
Imperial Economic Conference, 1932; Report of the Conference (Ottawa,1932) 38.

12.   See F.A. Knox, Dominion Monetary Policy, 1929-1934, (Ottawa;
Royal Commission on Dominion-Provincial Relations, 1939), 30-3.

13.   The seasonally adjusted index of current loans fell from 107.1 in
October 1932 to 94.8 in May 1933 and, after a slight rise, to a trough of 91.3 in
July 1934.   The index of call loans in Canada fell from 88.4 in April 1932 to a
trough of 67.7 one year later.

14.   The impact of the legislation had been unfavourable.   Both the government bond and foreign exchange markets reacted adversely, " apparently under the
impression that the government had succumbed to the pressure of those within
Canada who urged inflation" Knox, Dominion Monetary Policy, 1929-1934, 30.

15.   While the seasonally adjusted index of security holdings reached a
trough in March 1930, the combined total of these holdings and loans in Canada
did not reach a trough until July 1934.
        Throughout the period under study, the relative importance of current
loans in bank assets decreased while that of securities increased.   This tendency became particularly marked after 1930. Among the reasons for this phenomenon were:
the growing tendency of corporations to finance working capital out of retained
savings, the greater ease with which corporations could issue bonds and securities
arising from the increasing size of the average corporation and also the widening of
the post-war capital market, the growing demand for social services and hence
increased supplies of government bonds to be marketed, and the increasing importance
of such industries as newsprint, manufacturing and mining where larger corporations
able to finance themselves predominated. Cf.J.D. Gibson, " The Trend of Bank
Loans and Investments in Canada," Canadian Investment and Foreign Exchange
Problems, ed. J.F. Parkinson (Toronto, 1940), chap XII, 154-60.

16.   The seasonally adjusted index of Dominion notes in the hands of the
public rose after November 1932; that of demand deposits after January 1933. While
the unadjusted total of demand and notice deposits in Canada reached a trough of
$1,825 million in July 1932, no strong subsequent rise developed; it was $1,829
million in January 1933 and $1,827 million one year later.

17. The scatter diagram Fig. 2 reveals a definite downward shift of the
consumption function in 1933-4. It resulted from the shift of the function relating
consumption to personal disposable income. Thus the decrease in the average propensity to consume in 1934 does not merely reflect an upward movement along a

stable consumption schedule. (Again, when consumption is lagged three months
behind personal disposable income, no significant shift occurs at this time.)

18. Nor did a strong rise of the marginal propensity to consume effect the
up-turn. Obtained from the yearly changes in revised real consumption and real
GNP it fell from .61 in 1932 to .30 in 1933, and rose slightly to .36 in 1934.
The marginal propensity obtained from personal disposable income, perhaps a better
measure of any psychological propensity, rose from .86 in 1932 to .97 in 1933 and
fell sharply to .60 in 1934.

19. Personal saving rose from minus $113 million in 1933 to plus $12
million in 1934. The seasonally adjusted index of notice deposits reached a trough
in January 1934.

20. In addition, the production of producers' goods rose after December
1932, while the production of consumers' goods fell until February 1933. Again,
in so far as retail sales may be taken as a criterion of consumption demand, the
expected lead of the up-turn of sales before the up-turn of physical output of
consumers' goods is not in evidence. The acceleration principle related to domestic
consumption alone does not seem to explain the up-turn of the production of
producers' goods since this up-turn occurred before the revival of consumers' goods
production.

21. Even in 1933 new investment rose in seven industrial sectors: primary
woods operations; mining; rubber, leather, and tobacco and their products; primary
textiles; chemicals; private electric railways; and commercial services (Department
of Trade and Commerce, Private and Public Investment in Canada, 1926-1951.
Ottawa, 1951, 155, 158f., 163,172, 179), although certainly not all this investment
was induced. Gross domestic investment rose from $146 million in 1932 to $157
million in 1933, largely because of the fall of inventory disinvestment from $216
million to $ 82 million (D.B.S., National Accounts, Income and Expenditure,
1926 - 1950, Ottawa, 1952, 46).

22. The yield on Dominion of Canada long-term bonds fell from 4.49 per
cent in 1932 to 4.08 and 3.57 per cent in the next two years, compared with the
fall from 3.68 to 3.31 and 3.12 on United States Government long-term bonds. In
addition, this fall was sharper than in 1921. In the three years 1921 to 1923 long-
term yield in Canada fell by .09, .50, and .28 percentage points compared with
.41, .51, and .31 in the three years 1933 to 1935.

23.   This conclusion is supported by the fact that corporation bond prices,
common stock prices, and preferred stock prices, all reached their cyclical troughs
and experienced definite cyclical tendencies in exactly the same months as the
series on pure yield. Pure long-term yield had a slightly higher value in January
1932 (4.77 per cent) than in June 1932 (4.76 per cent) but no sharp decline materialized until after the latter date.

24.   National Accounts, Income and Expenditure, 1926-1950, 46. Construction and gross domestic investment rose 5 and 85 per cent in 1922 (M.R.B.S., April 1944, 38).

25.   A lag would be expected, of course, between the time when the fall of yield might have induced entrepreneurs to undertake new investment and the actual turning out of the investment goods. But since the timing of the business cycle trough has been ascertained by taking the median of the troughs of the various output indexes (and not of entrepreneurial plans for increased output), favourable influences from the rate of interest are pertinent here only if the resulting increase in output occurred before the business cycle trough.

26.   While the net debt of the Dominion government rose by $84 million, $114 million and $221 million in the year 1931 to 1933, the deficit of all three levels of government fell from $311 million to $277 million and $174 million. Thus no strong forces making for revival are indicated if one believes that government dissaving can effect an up-turn.

27.   Appendix C, Table XVI. The index of efficiency of production per wage earner in manufacturing industries fell from 151.9 in 1931 to 146.9 in 1932, and rose only to 147.2 in 1933.

28.   Nevertheless these wage reductions made possible many small jobs.

29.   The indexes of wage rates of common factory labour and miscellaneous factory trades fell from peaks of 188.2 and 202.3 in 1930 to troughs of 168.1 and 175.7 in 1933; those of the metal and building trades from peaks of 186.6 and 203.2 in 1930 to troughs of 168 and 154.8 in 1934.

30.   While construction costs fell by 20.4 per cent, 1929-33, the index of rent fell 24.4 per cent from its peak in 1930 to its trough in 1934.

31.   The annual index of efficiency in manufacturing industries, as measured by output per employee, is used here as a first approximation.

32. Appendix C, Table XIV. Automobile production, which rose 78 per cent in 1923-9, declined 21 per cent in 1929-37 despite improvement of models to stimulate sales.

33. Electric power, newsprint, and lead production rose by 54, 35 and 26 per cent in 1929-37 contrasted with 122, 115 and 194 per cent in 1923-9.

34. This fact explains in part why the Canadian expansion of the 30's was disappointing. Current gross domestic investment was $741 million in 1937 compared with $1391 million in 1929. GNP per capita was only $485 in 1937 compared with $615 in 1928.

35. Canada's cyclical trough came in March 1933. A.F. Burns and W.C. Mitchell have derived the following troughs (Measuring Business Cycles, New York, 1946, 78f):

France	July,	1932
Great Britain	August,	1932
Germany	August,	1932
United States	March,	1933

36. Seven major series rose more sharply in the United States and five in Canada. Of the three over-all aggregates, the two national income series rose more rapidly in Canada but GNP more rapidly in the United States. Moreover, the increases in most of the series were roughly of the same order of magnitude. Thus the early Canadian upswing was roughly as intense as the American and hence as most of those abroad. (Appendix C. Table XII.) On the other hand, the early British upswing was not as rapid as either the American or the Canadian. Only one of the thirteen series common to both Britain and Canada reveals a sharper increase in Britain. (The change in Canadian wholesale prices was again somewhere between that of British and that of American prices. This behaviour has been found in each of the instances measured in this study.)

37. Canada's trough came at the same time and her upswing was as intense as the American and thus as most of those abroad; the cyclical troughs in Canada's total exports and imports came in the same month (February 1933) and those in Canadian-American trade flows came in the same month (February 1933). British and French up-turns preceded the Canadian, and Canada's exports to Britain and France rose (after January 1931 and August 1932) before her imports from them (after January 1933).

38. Appendix C., Table XIII. All categories of exports to the United States rose in or before April 1933. Only two types of exports to the United Kingdom and three to Other Countries did not contribute to the Canadian up-turn.

39. The percentage export changes in the following table evidence the relative importance of exports to Britain and the United States to the Canadian upturn.

	U.K.	U.S.	O.C.	Total.
1932	+ 7.2	. . .	. . .	. . .
1933	+26.2	+ 4.7	. . .	+ 7.5
1934	+24.5	+27.7	+ 12.6	+21.8

40. Freight receipts from Britain rose from $5 million in 1932 to $8 million and $11 million in the next two years, and those from the United States from $25 million to $28 million and $32 million. Those from Other Countries rose from $7

million in 1931 to $8 million, $8 million, and $9 million in the next three years.

41.   Occasionally, however, when a premium rose on the price of some types of gold, temporary market conditions induced exports to overseas countries.

Chapter Seven

1.   Obviously this is not a generalization that all such countries must have their turning-points preceding those abroad, nor that such a phenomenon is the most probable. The point is that such a pattern is possible.

2.   The British textile industry tends to slump relatively early (see W.H. Beveridge, Full Employment in a Free Society, London, 1944, 297-300,306.)

3.   Unfortunately data are not available on the alterations in canons of liquidity prescribed by the banks for collateral so that a closer testing is not possible.

4.   R.G. Hawtrey, Capital and Employment (London, 1937), 117.

5.   Nor did any significant correlation of stocks of manufactured goods with bank rates occur in 1930-4 when these rates became more flexible, in so far as the limited data I have been able to secure from the banks are a realiable guide.

6.   The only justification for this contention would be that Say's law held, but such an assumption is obviously untenable as a statement of reality.

7.   Ibid., 248

8.   R.G. Hawtrey, Currency and Credit (3rd ed., London, 1927),135.

9.   Ibid., 138 and "London and the Trade Cycle," American Economic Review, Supplement, XIX, 1 (March 1929), 71.

10.   Currency and Credit, 139.

11.   "London and the Trade Cycle," 71. See also The Art of Central Banking (London, 1932), 203f. It should be noted that Hawtrey's theory of the relative timing of the pre-war British cycle is diametrically opposed to Schumpeter's.

12.   If it could be assumed that low discount rates induced dealers to stock up mainly goods of countries producing raw materials, then the expansionary effect might well be greater abroad than in Britain, especially if the prices of the imported raw material are raised. Such price changes are obviously an important agency for the transmission of cyclical change.

13.   I do not mean to imply, however, that the volume of bank credit may not be an important determinant of the volume of activity.

14. W. Edwards Beach, British International Gold Movements and Banking Policy, 1881-1913 (Cambridge, 1935).

15.   Ibid., 170

16.   Moreover, his conclusion has been accepted by C.P. Kindleberger (International Short-term Capital Movements, New York, 1937, 143) and P.B. Whale ("The Working of the Pre-War Gold Standard," Economica, IV, N.S., no. 13, February 1937, 26).

17.   Beach, British International Gold Movements, 172.

18.   Except for 1931-2, bank loans behaved perversely; they aggravated the disequilibria rather than alleviated them. There is no evidence, of course, that the banks deliberately intended to thwart the mechanism of adjustment. The persistent slow decline of bank loans in the first half of the upswing may largely reflect the banks' rescue of firms from their difficulties inherited from the 1920-1 inventory boon and débâcle and also a small demand for loans as business as a whole picked up very slowly. The banks no doubt lent only to "good business risks" in the latter half of the upswing although some banks contributed more actively to the continual upsurge of loans than others.

19.   Cf. Kindleberger, International Short-term Capital Movements, 138, 140ff.

20.   See Whale, "The Working of the Pre-War Gold Standard," passim.

21.   Actually Hawtrey had stressed in some contexts the role of changes in income and purchasing power. See especially Currency and Credit, 76-82, on income alterations tending to close a gap in the balance of payments caused by crop variations, and 83ff. on shifts of purchasing power contributing to the mechanism of capital transfer.

22.   See Chapter I, section I. Kindleberger gives some reasons why cyclical fluctuations abroad may have had a larger amplitude of fluctuation than those in England. International Short-term Capital Movements, 141.

23.   Beach recognises that the importance of income variations in affecting the behaviour of international accounts is not properly stressed in the so-called classical model but has not made the necessary qualifications. He admits that shifts in demand schedules " are likely to be more important than the elasticity of demand, when price and income levels are changing" but appears to recognise only those shifts in demand connected with fluctuations in the volume of foreign loans and with "price changes in general" (British International Gold Movements, 171). Perhaps it was this ignoring of shifts of demand resulting from purchasing power variations based on fluctuations of the current account and not necessarily connected with price movements that led Beach to his first criticism of the modified classical model.

24. Ibid., 172

25. Currency and Credit, 115.

26. Ibid., 116,168.

27. Beach, British International Gold Movements, 172.

28. Changes of "purchasing power" may be more appropriate here than "price changes."

29. Though neither may be the "independent variable" if they both result largely from some third force such as the relative strength of investment or in general activity at home and abroad and if this phrase be reserved for such a prime mover. In the empirical chapters certain accounts have been selected as being the "major factor" or "independent variable" in the international accounts, i.e., the factor within the international accounts themselves which appeared to have played a dominant role.

30. British International Gold Movements, 180.

31. Ibid., 173. Laughlin, de Lavaleye, and Marshall had advanced this theory previously but with reference to price levels. Without short-term capital flow data, Beach was unable to test this theory empirically. He shows that English discount rates rose in prosperity (p. 103) while internal demand for coin used up the specie imports and also lowered the gold stock of the Bank of England (pp. 77f.); but this by no means proves his thesis.

32. Only in three of the thirteen years studied did a positive correlation exist between the price of the Canadian dollar in New York and the annual estimates of short-term capital movements. The monthly short-term capital estimates (excluding monetary gold) yield a positive correlation with the price of the Canadian dollar in New York in 54.5 per cent of the fluctuations in 1921-33; the monthly current account and monthly capital account balances in 60.3 and 43.2 per cent of the fluctuations respectively. In the annual data on net sales of outstanding securities only seven of the thirteen fluctuations in 1921-33 indicated an increase of net sales (or decrease of net purchases from abroad) when the Canadian dollar depreciated.

33. These are exceptions only when the absolute change and not the direction of movement is considered. Thus, for example, in 1922 a credit of $27 million occurred when a debit would be expected; but the credit was $144.4 million in 1921.

34. Cf. J.F. Parkinson, "The Foreign Exchange Rate and the Mechanism of International Adjustment, "Canadian Investment and Foreign Exchange Problems (Toronto, 1940) Chap. VI, 76f., and Arthur I. Bloomfield, "The Significance of Outstanding Securities in the International Movement of Capital," C.J.E.P.S.,

VI, no. 4 (November 1940), 513f.
        Still it cannot be said that fluctuations of the exchange rate were by
any means the major determinant of the fluctuations in the sales and purchases
of outstanding securities. Market psychology (cf. D.B.S., The Canadian Balance of
International Payments: A Study of Methods and Results, Ottawa, 1939, 133f.)
and the relative speed of the movements of the business cycle at home and abroad
seem to have been more important determinants.

        35.   It should be noted that Hawtrey's ingenious extensions of the classical
analysis were based primarily on the assumption of an elastic monetary circulation
such as appears to have existed in Canada on the whole during the period of the
Finance Act. Thus the basic assumption of Hawtrey's analysis was fulfilled in
Canada but perhaps not in the two cases studied by Beach.

        36.   Hawtrey's merchandise model is only partially substantiated, of course,
because the long-term capital account seems to have been the dominant factor in
the international accounts during the downswing.

        37.   Because of the stress on "artificial" credit creation the bank rate seems
to be the one to compare with the real or equilibrium rate. Monetary over investment
theorists usually postulate a relatively close connection between short- and long-term
rates of interest but the former is generally regarded as the key determinant. Cf.
D.H. Robertson, "Industrial Fluctuation and the Natural Rate of Interest", Economic
Journal, XLIV, No. 176 (December 1934), 650f.

        38.   F.A. Hayek, Monetary Nationalism and International Stability (London,
1937).

        39.   R. Nurkse, Internationale Kapitalbewegungen (Vienna, 1935), 209. The
weakest point of his theoretical model is his contention that capital imports
necessarily contribute to cyclical expansion and capital exports to contraction.
Obviously capital exports may stimulate activity in the lending country since the
demand for its products depends upon the volume of its currency possessed by
foreigners. Cf. B. Ohlin, Interregional and International Trade (Cambridge, 1933),
429n., and J. Viner, Studies in the Theory of International Trade (London, 1937),
434f. Whether capital movements are deflationary or expansionary depends, of course,
upon what is actually done with the funds compared with what would otherwise have
been done with them.
        In this connection it should be noted that capital-importing countries
need not be depressed by capital imports under paper standard conditions. (Contrast
G. Haberler, Prosperity and Depression, Geneva, 1941, 447, and P.B. Whale
"International Trade in the Absence of an International Standard," Economica, III,
N.S., no. 9, February 1936, 31f.) Even though no counter-balancing movements
of gold or short-term capital are present to induce expansion, the additional home
investment induced by the utilization of the foreign savings in some sector of the

economy might more than offset the deflationary effect of increased merchandise imports. Since the supply of local bank credit would presumably be relatively elastic under paper standard conditions, such induced investment might well be important.

40. Cf. L. Robbins, The Great Depression (London, 1935), 44.

41. It must be pointed out that both Robbins and Nurkse now seem to have a much more eclectic view of business cycle causation than might be construed from their volumes referred to here.

42. No doubt the fall in bond prices in 1920 and the subsequent rise influenced flotations during the months when changes were occurring, especially when prices were falling. The point here, however, is that no turning-point of general activity was effected by bond price fluctuations.

43. Moreover, Cassel's stress on investment and technical progress appears to be consistent with the 1921 up-turn phenomena. In addition the pattern of the Canadian upswing appears to resemble somewhat that in Cassel's theory. Its two parts are reminiscent of Cassel's "period of the beginning of the advance" and "the trade boom proper." Similarly, the yearly increments of wages and salaries were substantially smaller during the first stage of the upswing than those of business income; and the opposite held true in the second phase. In accordance with Cassel's doctrine also, wages and salaries rose in the peak year, 1929, while profits fell.

44. The conclusion that the 1933 up-turn was not assisted by any long-term capital import holds only in so far as one can reason from the algebraic sum. Exports of new issues of Canadian securities actually rose by $30 million in 1933 while the net balance of the long-term capital account fell from a credit of $55 million to a debit of $41 million. If one could show that the $30 million was invested in a strategic sector and induced much additional investment and that the various other long-term capital flows were unimportant, then a net expansionary stimulus might be found here. But no such evidence has been found.

45. G. Wood, Borrowing and Business in Australia: A Study of the Correlation between Imports of Capital and Changes in National Prosperity (London, 1930).

46. See chap. V, section II.

47. Further evidence that the long-term capital account was more a resultant than a determinant of the business cycle is the usual lag of this account behind GNP as indicated by the predominantly anti-clockwise pattern of the scatter with GNP on the horizontal axis.

48. See chap. I, section II.

49. Preferred and common combined. The peak of common stock issues came in 1930 but almost as many were floated in 1929.

50. Cf. Carl Iversen, Aspects of the Theory of International Capital Movements (2nd ed., Copenhagen, 1936), 73.

51. See Beach, British International Gold Movements, 170, and H. D. White, The French International Accounts, 1880-1913 (Cambridge, Mass., 1933), 218ff.

52. Chang has found that British cyclical fluctuations were less intense than those abroad during the inter-war period and that British capital exports were correlated positively with the British trade cycle. "The British Balance of Payments, 1924-1938," Economic Journal, LVII, no. 228 (December 1947), 482 n and 487.

53. White, The French International Accounts, 220f. Cf. also Folke Hilgerdt, "Foreign Trade and the Short Business Cycle," Economic Essays in Honour of Gustav Cassel (London, 1933), 279.

54. Cf. A. I. Bloomfield, "The Mechanism of Adjustment of the American Balance of Payments: 1919-1929," Quarterly Journal of Economics, LVII (May 1943), 333-77, which was drawn to my attention in 1950, for a somewhat similar hypothesis to explain the co-variation of American trade and long-term capital balances. Bloomfield actually stresses domestic business fluctuations as "the common influence" but occasionally makes use of the hypothesis of American business fluctuations being "more intense than those in the rest of the world" (p. 376).

55. White, The French International Accounts, 218-21.

56. Ibid., 220 f. The correlation between French activity and capital exports appears slightly stronger than in White's conclusions when the direction of movement is considered. If the 11 cases when no yearly change occurs in the crude measure of business activity are omitted, 15 of the remaining 22 years reveal a positive correlation between the level of French activity and capital exports, i.e., over 68 per cent of these cases.

57. In correspondence Professor Viner has stated that his "scepticism was confined to the existence of a single and a priori ascertainable cyclical pattern applicable to different cycles and to different countries."

58. Cf. White, The French International Accounts, 221.

59. Moreover, the flow of long-term capital would only conform to the relative rates of expansion under the assumption that interest rates, stock prices,

and profit rates are directly correlated with the speed of the business expansion. In so far as this is not true, for example, if an inordinate stock market boom occurred in a country with a slow expansion, the long-term capital flows would become more complex.

60. Cf. A.I. Bloomfield, Capital Imports and the American Balance of Payments 1934-39 (Chicago, 1950) 304-8.

61. The net sales and purchases of outstanding securities must also be considered here because they include, to some extent, redemptions again but not of Canadian securities originally sold abroad.

62. See D.C. MacGregor, "Tendencies in Canadian Investment", Canadian Investment and Foreign Exchange Problems, Chap. XXIII 279 f.

63. Cf. R.B. Bryce, " The Effects on Canada of Industrial Fluctuations in the United States, " C.J.E.P.S., V, no. 3 (August 1939), 384.

64. Moreover, the 1927 American recession and resulting decrease in capital supply may help account for the decrease in new Canadian issues there that year.

65. See Taussig's lucid account of how successive international credit cycles brought repeated crises to the United States and Argentina when they were borrowers. F.W. Taussig, International Trade (New York, 1927), 130.

66. For example: " To repeat, it all just happened. One can make out nothing in the nature of an ordered sequence, of conformity to rule or to reasoning." Ibid., 332.

67. Though, of course, it may not be applicable to the cases Taussig studied.

68. The remaining gap may, of course, grow larger if these mechanisms of adjustment are not powerful enough.

69. But a more important reason for the low level of personal income was the unsatisfactory market for exports, especially for wheat. Farm purchasing power fell 59 per cent, 1920-4 (W.A. Mackintosh, The Economic Background of Dominion-Provincial Relations, Ottawa, 1939, 39). The terms of trade had been against exporters vis-a-vis the sheltered industries and this was aggrevated by the high ratio of fixed costs to income.
    The cessation of wage and salary cuts might have prevented consumption from falling even further in 1923-4. According to Professor D.C. MacGregor, however the wonder is that larger wage cuts were not needed since wages were still high

relative to wholesale prices. Large-scale emigration to the United States may explain in part why wages were not cut further and may account in part for the fall in consumption.

70. It is interesting to note that the fluctuations of the Canadian consumption function seem to conform with J.S. Duesenberry's "ratchet effect" (Income, Saving and the Theory of Consumer Behaviour, Cambridge, Mass., 1949, 114ff.) in so far as declines in consumption were usually along a higher function. Cf. F. Modigliani, "Fluctuations in the Saving-Income Ratio: A Problem in Economic Forecasting," Studies in Income and Wealth, vol. XI (New York, 1949), 394.

71. Similarly, the allowance of a possible lag of one year of investment behind the rate of growth of consumption expenditure does not improve the fit significantly throughout.

72. I.e., much of the investment was not determined by current consumption or current income changes although its final purpose was production for consumption in some future period.

73. Since consumption expenditure usually lagged behind GNP by from five to seven months the conclusion that much of the investment was autonomous is further strengthened.

74. In so far as there was a positive shift of the consumption function in 1929, the case for the contention that the boom halted itself because of the functional relationship of consumption to income is weakened. Of course, the gap between consumption and income was too large as the boom progressed.

75. There was probably no overinvestment in hotels, most office buildings, stores, and perhaps houses.

76. J.M. Keynes, "The German Transfer Problem," Economic Journal, XXXIX, no. 153 (March 1929), 6.

77. Viner sides with neither belief, sees "no apparent a priori reason why the dependence should not be as much in one direction as the other" (Studies in the Theory of International Trade, 364), but considers historical fact to confirm the orthodox doctrine with long-term capital movements as the major disturbing force (ibid., 365). He has pointed out in correspondence that the current account may be potentially an independent variable but may require, to make it operative, willingness abroad to lend and also willingness to borrow.

78. Ohlin, Interregional and International Trade, 383f.

79. Cf. Alfred E. Kahn, Great Britain in the World Economy (London, 1946), 7f.

80. In ascertaining the major independent variable, it has been found useful (1) to correlate the partial balances of the international accounts with the exchange rate and (2) to compute monthly balance of payments estimates as a more secure test of this correlation.

81. In the very early stages of a "new" country's development the capital account may well be relatively much more important, and hence dominate the other international account items and be responsible for major exchange rate changes. With a large stock of capital in place and adequate internal savings, the situation may be quite different.

82. The mechanism of adjustment with respect to gaps in the current account balance appears applicable also to gaps in the long-term capital account providing the words " purchasing power" be substituted for "income" throughout (since capital movements cannot be said to give rise directly to shifts of income). Demand schedules may shift not only because of changes in income but also because of increased bank or foreign credits.

83. See, for example, J.M. Keynes, The Means to Prosperity (London, 1933), 35ff.

84. One-fifth to one-quarter would be a more realisitic value for Canada's marginal propensity to import.

85. A.J. Brown, "Trade Balances and Exchange Stability, " Oxford Economic Papers, no. 6 (April 1942) 57-75.

Appendix A

1. For sources of yearly data see Chap. II n 6.

2. The trade data from 1920 to March 1927 are from the Monthly Report of the Trade of Canada (Ottawa), thereafter from the Quarterly Report of the Trade of Canada (Ottawa).

3. Merchandise import and export "totals for March are always greater than those for April. March figures must include all entries at all ports to the close of the fiscal year (March 31). In all other months the records are closed at Ottawa on the last day of the month. Late import and export entries (which in the case of the great, but distant, port of Vancouver, may cover four or five days' business at the end of each month) are regularly included in totals for the succeeding month. April totals include nothing for March, while they are short some amounts carried

forward into May." Condensed Preliminary Report on the Trade of Canada, 1929 (Ottawa, 1929), 21.

4. This is widely recognized in the export of wheat. Cf., for example, R.S. Sayers, Modern Banking (2nd ed., Oxford, 1947) 48.

5. G.F. Towers, Financing Foreign Trade (Montreal, 1927), 10.

6. D.B.S., The Canadian Balance of International Payments: A Study of Methods and Results (Ottawa, 1939), 187.

7. The greatest divergence was $0.4 million.

8. Ibid., 87, for estimates of in-transit traffic.

9. Ibid., 80.

10. Preliminary Estimates of Tourist Expenditures 1944 (Ottawa, 1945) 8.

11. Canada's International Tourist Trade, 1943 (Ottawa, 1944) 8, gives the figures for 1938-43. For 1937 see ibid., 1926-1942 (Ottawa, 1944) 36.

12. Ibid., 1926-1942, 40.

13. Ibid., 1943, 5. In 1937-9 automobile travellers made 52,51, and 51 per cent of the total American tourist expenditures in Canada.

14. Preliminary Estimates of Tourist Expenditures 1944, 8.

15. Canada's International Tourist Trade, 1926-1942, 36.

16. Correspondence with C.D. Blyth, Chief, International Payments Branch, D.B.S., dated April 26, 1947.

17. See Canada's International Tourist Trade, 1926-1942, 36.

18. Correspondence with Blyth.

19. The Canadian Balance of International Payments: A Study of Methods and Results, 97f.

20. Correspondence with Blyth.

21. This group of dividends was not so important in the earlier part of the period under study as later.

22.   Correspondence with Blyth.

23.   See J. Viner, Canada's Balance of International Indebtness, 1900-13 (Cambridge, 1924), 30-4.

24.   These balances were derived by deducting such liabilities as (1) deposits elsewhere than in Canada, (2) deposits by and balances due banks in the United Kingdom and elsewhere, and (3) bills payable from such assets as (1) foreign government and bank notes, (2) amounts due from foreign banks, (3) public securities other than Canadian, (4) call and short loans elsewhere, and (5) current loans elsewhere than in Canada. Unfortunately these series fail to correspond exactly to those desirable for balance of payments purposes since some local business done by foreign branches of Canadian banks is not eliminated completely. The Canadian Bankers' Association compiles a more exact formulation on a yearly basis but there is no way of distributing these sums accurately over the various months.

25.   From 1928 on. From the Chronicle in 1921-7.

26.   Cf. F.A. Knox, Excursus, " Canadian Capital Movements and the Canadian Balance of International Payments, 1900-1934" in H. Marshall, F.A. Southard, Jr., and K.W. Taylor, Canadian-American Industry (New Haven, 1936), 323 f. This procedure agrees with D.B.S. practice up to 1932.

27.   Ibid.

28.   The Canadian Balance of International Payments: A Study of Methods and Results, 202.

Appendix B

1.   Figures for fiscal year 1933 were obtained from Trade of Canada, Fiscal Year 1933 (Ottawa) and those for 1920 from S. Smith, D.B.S., letter dated May 20, 1948.

2.   The 1920-1 figures of this series are not strictly comparable with the rest because of minor alterations in the Department of National Revenue categories. No correction was attempted for our computations since the 1920 figures were not available in detail and since complete correction was not even possible for 1921.

3.   A more refined computation should perhaps include interest and dividends and "other current payments." Because of their relative stability they have not been included.

INDEX

www.ingramcontent.com/pod-product-compliance
Lightning Source LLC
Chambersburg PA
CBHW051755200326
41597CB00025B/4564